THE FICTION OF JOHN O'HARA

Critical Essays in English and
American Literature No. 7

*The quotations in this volume are used with
the permission of John O'Hara, for which both author
and publisher are grateful.*

EDWARD RUSSELL CARSON: # The

Fiction

of

John O'Hara

UNIVERSITY OF PITTSBURGH PRESS

Library of Congress Catalog Card Number: 61–9397

Contents

I. Introduction

T HE "GIBBSVILLE" or "Lantenengo County" novels and stories by John O'Hara are set in and around the fictional city of Gibbsville, Pennsylvania. They are, in order of publication, *Appointment in Samarra, A Rage to Live, Ten North Frederick, From the Terrace,* and *Ourselves to Know.*

Pottsville, a city of Pennsylvania, U.S., the county seat of Schuylkill County; on the Schuylkill River, 90 mi. N.W. of Philadelphia. It is served by the Lehigh Valley, the Reading and the Pennsylvania railways. The population in 1950 was 23,640; in 1940 it was 24,530 by the Federal Census. It has a picturesque location (627 ft. above sea level) at the gap made by the river through Sharp Mountain and is in the midst of the southern ("Schuylkill") region of the anthracite coal field. Besides its large coal-mining interests, it has railroad shops and a variety of manufacturing industries, including textiles, aluminum and steel fabrication. The city operates under a commission form of government.

The first white family that settled there was massacred by the Indians in Aug. 1780. Permanent settlement dates from about 1795, and soon after that an iron furnace was set up. In 1804 this furnace was bought by John Potts, founder of the borough. Coal was discovered in 1807.

The town was laid out in 1816, incorporated as a borough in

1

1828, became the county seat in 1851 and was chartered as a city in 1911.[1]

Aside from considerations of locale, what sets these works apart from O'Hara's other novels and collections of short stories is that the Gibbsville novels comprise a more noticeably auto-biographic outlet for the author's personal experience. O'Hara does not alter the situations presented by life in Northeastern Pennsylvania any more than is necessary for the sake of "art." "You're on pretty sound ground if you start out with a life you know about," [2] says O'Hara, who makes a deliberate attempt in these novels to select from actual experience the characters and situations which appear in his fiction.[3]

As to style, there is another difference in the novels from that in other writings of O'Hara. The novelist desires only to describe with the intensest attention to descriptive detail just how individuals from every range of the Gibbsville populace, regardless of their social station, live from one day to the next throughout indefinite time. The photographic precision of the still-life painter is O'Hara's method. He attempts to display a communal *modus vivendi* as it affects each individual character being described. In *Ten North Frederick*, he says:

> The biographer has certain rights and duties and among them is the right, which is also a duty, to say that at such-and-such a point the biographee's life left one phase and entered another. It is not the same as saying that a change occurred overnight, for there are few occurrences—if there are any—that bring about radical and quick changes in the lives of human beings. Change is almost always fluid; rapidly fluid, or slowly fluid; but even major events in a human life do not make the overnight personality changes that they are often said to make. Marriage, parenthood, the suc-cessful culmination of an enterprise, a severe punishment, a dread-ful accident resulting in blindness, a frightening escape from danger, an exhilarating emotional experience, the unexpected report of a five-inch gun, a sudden view of something loathsome, the realization of a great major chord, an abrupt alteration in a human relationship—they all take time, to be absorbed by the soul, no matter how infinitesimally brief a time they took in oc-curring or in being experienced. Only death itself causes that overnight change, but then of course there is no morning.

To carry further the analogy with the visual arts, O'Hara examines life closely in order better to determine what has gone wrong in a life situation as well as what one may do in order to avoid or avert a repetition of the mishap. This is the intention of the genre-painter whose naturalist inclination is to display his subject matter openly and at close range. The naturalist novelist (i.e., Emile Zola, Thomas Hardy, or Frank Norris) also means to show specific events with verisimilitude against a background ruled by certain determinants. These determinants may consist of social injustice, physical disease, or the imperturbability of a hostile universe. Naturalistic agents for O'Hara, however, exist in sexual attraction, economic deprivation, but most of all, the rigidity of social class lines. "The cruel side of social snobbery is O'Hara's main theme," [4] says Edmund Wilson. The tragedy endured by a character in any of the first three "Gibbsville" novels is in proportion to how he is either prevented from rising on the social ladder, or how he must remain aloof from the things he most desires because of "station." This consideration will deter one from either "betraying his class" or being censured by his circle of family and acquaintances. Such characters as Joe Chapin or Grace Tate will never obtain what they desire most of all—particularly speaking, satisfaction of political ambition or satisfaction in a love relationship. These people realize too well, as members of their economic and social class, how they must live in terms of this confinement. They may once or twice in their lives explosively flaunt the *mores* of Gibbsville, but never will they depart from them for good.

What makes John O'Hara's vision of such people exclusively his own is that their suffering is never violent or incredible. There exists in these three novels only the most ordinary (however intense) suffering of mundane and everyday reality. No one commits suicide in such novels, *A Rage to Live* and *Ten North Frederick* for example. Little of the Fitzgeraldian exuberance, as it is experienced on such a scale as in *The Great Gatsby* or *May Day*, appears in these novels. Here there exist only such typical problems as disappointment in love, death in one's immediate family, or failure in one's vocation. This emphasis upon the minutiae of ordinary experience is revealed visually and concretely. O'Hara's is the tragedy of the commonplace.

But, not to depart from O'Hara as social commentator— it is not enough merely to describe his characters' contemporaneous acts and thoughts. Their ancestry and private lives up to where the action begins also seem deeply relevant to O'Hara. This is why his reportage on his people's private careers includes such meticulous attention to matters of residence, schools and colleges attended, and the superficially social aspects of employment. In the novels on life in Lantenengo County it is not surprising that O'Hara should read at times like a social history of Gibbsville. He is as concerned with the genealogy of preceding generations as he is with the life of a character at the moment in which the character is being described.

Dr. English, for example, comes from one of the oldest families in Gibbsville:

> He was of Revolutionary stock. He wore a ring with an indistinguishable crest (he took it off when he operated). Adam English, one of his ancestors, had come to Gibbsville in 1804, two years after Gibbsville was refounded (Gibbsville was founded by Swedes in 1750, as nearly as anyone could make out; the Swedes had been massacred by the Leni Lenape Indians, and the Swedish name of the original settlement has been lost).[5]

By reporting not only on a person's present situation but also upon the lives of his family and ancestors, O'Hara is doing more than displaying his historical proficiency. Hereditary factors will thus not go unconsidered; in, for example, the case of Julian English, we are shown "how the suicide strain had skipped one generation to come out in the next." More important, however, is the effect of an individual's family history in determining his present social status. Of Katherine Doane Fliegler, the wife of Luther Fliegler, Julian English's business associate, O'Hara says:

> Her family had been in Gibbsville a lot longer than the great majority of people who lived on Lantenengo Street. She was a Doane, and Grandfather Doane had been a drummer boy in the Mexican War and had a Congressional Medal of Honor from the Civil War. Grandfather Doane had been a member of the School

Board for close to thirty years, before he died, and he was the only man in this part of the state who had a Congressional Medal of Honor.[6]

Such reference reinforces a character's capacity to represent, through his actions and thoughts, his class origins. To O'Hara, an individual can never escape the determinism of family background. He says: "I do a lot of family tree stuff. . . . I put down in great detail such things as births, dates, marriages and children. Some may be mentioned only once, but I'm a damn sight better off if I know all about them." [7]

The intricacies of middle-class "caste" distinction, then, are for John O'Hara what alcoholism, disease, or genetic disturbance would be for any European naturalist of the last century. To see O'Hara as "an Irishman who ate his heart out because he did not pass for society in the hard-coal region of Pennsylvania" [8] is to perceive in the man's work the motive for his exploitation of the realities of life in Gibbsville.

II. The Novels

W HAT DISTINGUISHES the Gibbsville novels as a group is (1) their restriction to Lantenengo County, Pennsylvania, (2) their emphasis upon class standing as social determinant, (3) their narrative clarity, (4) the pessimism with which O'Hara regards these issues.

O'Hara never wanders from recollections of the intimate experience of his own youth and middle age in Pottsville, rendered precisely in these novels and accorded as little revision as possible. The "Gibbsville" novels are, to a very large extent, sheer autobiography.[9] O'Hara has likewise elaborated on this matter in his book of essays, *Sweet and Sour*.

> The small town, like my invention Gibbsville, has it all; the entrenched, the strivers, the climbers, the rebellious. But the big town, by which I mean the Boston-Providence-New York-Philadelphia-Wilmington-Baltimore group, offers many more of the entrenched, the striving, the climbing and the rebelling to choose from. . . . [But] they both are tough to write about, or at least they are to me. . . . I have abundant information on their habits and their tribal customs, but they interest me so much it's hard for me to know when to stop.[10]

Pottsville, Pennsylvania, is, in all its reality, an endless source of material for O'Hara. In describing with the avidest attention possible any street or building or institution, he is using it either to create atmosphere or to lend credence to a character's motivation (in terms of either class consciousness or individual psychology), or simply to report it for its own sake and interest.

> The money was older on South Main and North Frederick. And in some cases, there was more of it. But it was not the amount of money that mattered in the scheme of things—Family X, living on Lantenengo Street, might be an old Gibbsville family with money, or might be a Gibbsville family with new money; but Family Y, living on North Frederick Street or South Main belonged to the old *and* the rich of Gibbsville.[11]

> She wore a tarnished blue straw hat with a wide black band, and her dress, which was open at the throat, was of navy-blue linen with a white leather belt, and she had on black silk stockings and white buckskin shoes with perforated black strapping across the vamp. Her only jewelry, besides her wedding and engagement rings, was a plain gold circle at the bottom of the V of her throat. She dressed like a member, belonging exactly to her class, with a Yale husband in the background, tennis and swimming for exercise, Protestantism for her religion, no extravagance in her character, and discontent never far from her contemplation.[12]

> Gibbsville moved up from the status of borough and became a third class city in 1911, but in 1930 the city still had less than 25,000 inhabitants (estimated 1930 population in the notebooks sent out by the Gibbsville banks to their depositors).[13]

O'Hara endlessly and remorselessly, with precision and minutest attention to detail, writes on his characters' education, clothing, speech and leisure habits in order that the reader may, after such an accretion of details, form his own conclusions on them not so much by inference as by sensing their personality gradually, objectively. "My characters have two patterns. One is superficial—clothes, schools, social positions, jobs. The other is psychological." [14] There is a sense of absolute correlation between Joe Chapin's having attended Hill School, Yale, and the law school of the University of Pennsylvania, "the traditional institution . . . in Gibbsville," [15] and Chapin's "seldom, if ever, appearing as counsel in a criminal court." [16] Small wonder that Edith Chapin, who "dressed like a member, belonging exactly to her class, with a Yale husband in the background," [17] will cause supreme unhappiness to her daughter in refusing her marriage to an Italian musician. O'Hara promotes his characterization by starting from the nucleus of a person's class insignia.

Nevertheless, no protagonist is any better off at the finish of any of the first three Gibbsville novels, no matter how much his "people have had money for much longer than the other people in this world," to quote from Grace Tate in *A Rage to Live*. Such a person may come of one of the "better" families in Gibbsville, or he may have to struggle along as a clerk, bookie, or jazz musician. He will never succeed "absolutely." More than any other inhibitory factor to keep him from so succeeding (this might be exemplified in the Gatsbian "Very Rich" of F. Scott Fitzgerald), will be the chimaera of class standing. Joe Chapin, as well as his butcher living in the downgraded section of Gibbsville, must face this reality and in its wake the doom that follows:

> There was only a small difference in their ages, an inconsiderable difference; and the two men had several matters in common. Each man had a son and a daughter, disappointing children. Both men had remote wives from whom they had never been separated. And now, with most of life gone in the one case and all of it gone in the other, it was too late for either man to realize his great ambition. The butcher had wanted to be heavy-weight prizefight champion of the world. Joe Chapin had always wanted to be President of the United States, and thought he ought to be.[18]

O'Hara's belief that in spite of a Gibbsvillian's belonging to the upper classes, in spite of his cultivation, wealth, and affluence, it is more likely than as not, that his life will be a failure. The protagonists of these three novels are bored, with no means of escaping their ennui except by momentary excitations or illusions of self-importance. As Julian English snubs his social inferiors, so Grace Tate maintains her amatory career, so Joe

Chapin drinks in the last years. None of these people is secure in a vocation or any "life's work" outside themselves. They may even become so absorbed in the purposelessness of their lives and the culture they represent as to become emotionally embittered and sterile—as is much the case with Mike Slattery, local politico whose delight it is to thwart Joe Chapin in the latter's Presidential aspirations, or Brock Caldwell, brother of Grace, whose only aspiration, for a career, is to compose a family genealogy in the belief that this will make him "literary." Such is their attention to diversion, to escaping life, and only accepting it on the visceral level or for what various moments in it "will supply [them] with some special self-respect." [19] Such is life in Gibbsville as seen through the eyes of John O'Hara—without hope, without salvation—once the trappings are removed. His people still "hardly know what they are or where they are headed." O'Hara's power, however, resides in his ability to show at the end of each novel, very clearly, what his people are and where they are headed—into the abyss of their own human condition.

More so than either of the two other novels in the Gibbsville epic, *Appointment in Samarra* constitutes O'Hara's object lesson in the cruel side of social snobbery. Julian English, the novel's protagonist, affronts a social climber at a dance. In turn, English himself is made the subject of ridicule for this error in taste. Two days later English commits suicide in despair.

Two varieties of social snobbery exist here. One is that of the "smoking room of the Lantenengo Country Club" and the other is the kind of censure exerted upon English by the middle class populace of Gibbsville who "collectively . . . presented a solid front of sound Pennsylvania Dutch and all that it implied. . . . What a pity it was that this business wasn't in the hands of one of their own men instead of being driven into the ground by a Lantenengo Street . . . wastrel." [20]

It is the snobbery of the Gibbsville *crème de crème* which displays first how the snobbery of Julian English's social milieu is turned back, ironically speaking, upon himself. Thus, English must suffer the same limitation as any person from another social group. He is reduced to humility by the censure of his clique. Whereas previously he might have relied upon his own social position in the "upper crust," he now becomes, like Harry Reilly (the Irish social sycophant whom English insults), equally despised. O'Hara's intention, morally, is to render the anguish of the socially snubbed. Julian English is the spokesman for most of us who at one time or another have been subject to the scorn of the *haute monde*—those of us who are excluded from the membership in the "better" college fraternity or the intimate circle of the Long Island garden party.

O'Hara's treatment of the finer points of class stratification appears meticulous, refined and precise in the expository part of his narrative. This is how O'Hara does it:

Any member of the club could come to the dance, but not everyone who came to the dance was really welcome in the smoking room. The smoking crowd always started out with a small number, always the same people. The Whit Hoffmans, the Julian Englishes, the Froggy Ogdens, and so on. They were the spenders and the socially secure, who could thumb their noses and not have to answer to anyone except their own families. There were about twenty persons in this group, and your standing in the younger set òf Gibbsville could be judged by the assurance with which you joined the nucleus of the smoking room crowd.

In like fashion, O'Hara depicts the wrath of Julian English against Harry Reilly, who is not a member of "the smoking room crowd."

Reilly had gone pretty far in his social climbing by being a "good fellow" and by "being himself," and by sheer force of the money which everyone knew the Reillys had. Reilly was on the greens committee and the entertainment committee, because as a golfer he got things done; he paid for entire new greens out of his own pocket, and he could keep a dance going till six o'clock by giving the orchestra leader a big tip. But he was not yet an officer in the Gibbsville Assembly.

In passages like these, O'Hara never falters in noting exactest gradations upon the social ladder.

Two days after insulting Reilly, English becomes subject to the same variety of malice and petty hatred which he has seen fit to exercise upon the Irishman. A fellow club member says to him, "I've done a lot of things in my life, but by Jesus if I ever sunk so low that I had to throw ice in a man's face and give him a black eye." The man's violence suggests a little ludicrously that English has committed an error in taste unbecoming to a member of the Gibbsville aristocracy.

That evening Julian English goes to a roadhouse with his wife. He becomes drunk and makes an attempt to sexually overcome Helene Hoffman, a singer there. By this time, he has done more than behave in bad taste, as with Reilly. He has attempted a major moral infraction. The chain of events is now speeding blindly toward the novel's fatal conclusion. When he appears at the Gibbsville Club for lunch the next day, he is insulted once more, and a quarrel ensues. Julian attempts a gentlemanly exit, but open violence follows:

> Froggy swung on him and Julian put up his open hand and the punch made a slight sound on his wrist, and hurt his wrist.
> "Gentlemen!"
> "Don't be a God damn fool," said Julian.
> "Well, then. Come on outside."
> "Gentlemen! You know the club rules." It was [the steward]. He stood in front of Froggy, with his back toward Froggy, facing Julian.

A lawyer then insults English, who insults him in return by calling him a "Polack war veteran and whoremaster."

> "Hey, you!" said the lawyer.
> "Aw," said Julian, finally too tired and disgusted with himself and everyone else. He took a step backwards and got into position, and then he let the lawyer have it, full in the mouth.

Julian attacks both the lawyer and Froggy. Infuriated, he hurls a carafe at still another man and runs for his car. His doom has been sealed. As he drives away, he suddenly realizes that Whit Hoffman, another friend, has detested him just as Froggy had—for a long time, quietly. This last experience has cost Julian any chance to make amends for his bad behavior, and his reputation in the town of Gibbsville is now at an ebb.

English arrives home to discover that his wife has deserted him. His final act of status derangement occurs during an attempt to seduce Alice Cartwright, a visiting journalist. Julian knows that he has by this time committed the local unpardonable sin of marital disloyalty. Sooner or later, he must face the enmity of all Gibbsville for his several moral infractions: The drink thrown into Harry Reilly's face, the Stage Coach Bar misadventure, the fight with Froggy and the lawyer, and the attempted seduction. Finally Julian English climbs into his car and dies of carbon monoxide poisoning.

Morally speaking, *Appointment in Samarra* attempts to display the psychological effect upon an individual of rejection by an in-group coterie. The didactic function of this novel is thus to warn the reader of the iniquity of pressing class distinctions to so extreme an issue. While John O'Hara may be a snob in his own right "as sensitive to social distinctions as any *arriviste* ever was," to quote from Delmore Schwartz,[21] O'Hara nevertheless takes time to display the person on the receiving end of class bigotry based upon a knowledge of "upper crust" ways. While one may detect in O'Hara's own motivation—at least as Delmore Schwartz sees it—an attempt to play vicariously the snob by writing about snobs themselves—*Appointment in Samarra* possesses a sympathy for English, and poses the question of just why such a calamity *was* necessary.

The novel of social criticism concerned with class mobility is no unusual phenomenon in American fiction. It has existed from Henry James through J. P. Marquand, as well as in the writers who constitute the chief influences upon O'Hara in this novel. "As for influences, here they are: Fitzgerald, Sinclair Lewis, Galsworthy, Tarkington, Owen Johnson, but chiefly Fitzgerald and Lewis." [22] Yet, in none of these authors exists so stringent an emphasis upon the suffering endured by the snubbed, except possibly in Fitzgerald's characterization of Gatsby. O'Hara, as Delmore Schwartz shows in *Partisan Review:*

. . . has a rich gift for social observation, for knowing how people are, what they are because of their background, and he has an acute, accurate ear which makes it possible for his characters to possess reality when they converse. But best of all, O'Hara is a snob; he is as sensitive to social distinctions as any *arriviste* ever was, and his snob-sensitivity provides him with inexhaustible energy for the transformation of observation into fiction. It was neither accident nor invention which made him call the scape-goat hero of his first novel, Julian English; for English is an Anglo-Saxon, he resents the Irish, he belongs to what is supposed to be the upper classes, and the tragic action which leads to his suicide is his throwing a drink in the face of a man with the choice name of Harry Reilly. It might just as well have been Murphy, O'Mara, or Parnell.[23]

Merely to pinpoint O'Hara as a social commentator, however, or chronicler of the ways of the *haute monde* is to fall short of the mark. Edmund Wilson, writing in 1941 in *The Boys in the Back Room,* says this about O'Hara, but also considerably more. While maintaining that "to read O'Hara on a fashionable bar or the Gibbsville Country Club is to be shown on the screen of a fluoroscope gradations of social prestige of which one had not before been aware," [24] Wilson also says, by way of certifying O'Hara's perception of class distinctions:

[There is] no longer any hierarchy here, either of cultivation or wealth; the people are all being shuffled about, hardly knowing what they are or where they are headed, but each is clutching some family tradition, some membership in a selective organization, some personal association with the famous, which will supply him with some special self respect . . . eventually, they all go under. They are snubbed, they are humiliated, they fail.[25]

O'Hara's characters cling to their illusions of superiority, their unvarying lot in the Gibbsville milieu, knowing only too well their own impotence and despair. Out of a hostility for this weakness and emotional apathy they will snub others and practice their kind of life before a mirror. Although O'Hara writes of "the cruel side of social snobbery" he does so from an even greater pessimism. It is a pessimism about the Very Rich, who perceive life only on the most sensate level possible, from one moment of indulgence to the next. As models for moral conduct, only a few of O'Hara's characters from the world of Julian English would suffice for most of us. It is a world which O'Hara describes with precision and insight. Because of O'Hara's restricting himself to describing only the visually real, the moral element in his novels becomes a thing of mundane but democratic necessity.

A Rage to Live is successful as a novel only insofar as one may define "novel" by one of two criteria. One is to consider such dynamic factors as change in character, or change in the author's own point of view toward his material from one point in the novel to another. *Appointment in Samarra* is such an example. On this score, *A Rage to Live* fails as a novel. But, there is a second, more static, method of writing a novel so that there is no change in any of the characters (though there is constant disclosure of them), and the author's unvaryingly dogmatic attitude toward his material exists only to hammer home this attitude by means of sheer repetition and volume. *A Rage to Live* causes one to marvel, as Harvey Breit has said,

> . . . at the sense of tumultuous life that Mr. O'Hara creates, both within the individual and within the various strata of the city. Intermittently one also marvels at his ear, at the rightness of the speech. One marvels at his fearlessness: the novel is ambitious in scope and vastness and weight . . . given the proper trims and disciplines, it would very nearly come off.[26]

The question of "proper trims and disciplines" is the big one not only for O'Hara, but for any serious novelist. My contention is that these "trims and disciplines" would only be valuable in a different type of novel from *A Rage to Live*.

The first way to approach John O'Hara's basically statis ideal in *A Rage to Live* involves a concern for the life which he depicts in its mundane reality. Thus, he deliberately avoids any consideration of change in the respective characters of Grace and Sidney Tate. In fact, as we shall see later, O'Hara's characterization of these two people is just as deliberately unchanging as are his descriptions of setting and locale.

O'Hara's concern for "local color" finds outlet in such descriptive passages as the following:

> It rained lightly on the morning of Wednesday, July 4, 1917, and the Festival Committee met to decide whether to postpone the Festival until the following Saturday. It was argued that Saturday was a better day than Wednesday, even if Wednesday did happen to be the Fourth. It also was argued by some of the Fort Penn businessmen that if the Festival was postponed until Saturday the merchants would be losing two and a half days that week: Wednesday the Fourth; the regular Thursday half holiday which the Merchants' Association members had decreed upon themselves; and now Saturday.

Here is recorded the conversation of "a mythical stranger to a mythical but observant citizen of Fort Penn," which describes Fort Penn anthropology in an intimately native manner:

> And let me say once and for all, our Pennsylvania Dutch couples can be mighty easy on the eye, at least when they're young. You take some of our young husbands and wives. . . . The boys—the third generation ones are getting taller and a good many of them are losing that straight line in the back of the head that makes them look like the Prussian Guard. Of course weight they still have to contend with, the boys and girls both. After they start making babies the girls get dumpy and the boys too. Sometimes a fellow wonders how they get near enough to have another baby, but they find a way, they find a way. And they're good eaters.

Local history in Lantenengo receives its due in the form of such descriptions as this:

> It was a Fort Penn custom every two years to elect George W. Walthour to the office of mayor. The custom had begun in 1905, when George, a handsome and already prosperous dentist of forty-two, got a kind of historical perspective on himself: he had been brought into the world during the afternoon of July 3, 1863, when George Gordon Meade repulsed George Edward Pickett's assault. The infant Walthour also was named George by his patriotic mother, but she had in mind George Washington because the day of her son's birth was so close to the Fourth of July.

There is probably no more telling and accurate description of the physical topography of the city of Fort Penn than this:

> The sidewalks of Fort Penn, state capital and county seat, always were occupied by more visitors than the streets of a town of equal size which had no governmental significance. The Fort Penn natives, as a consequence, were accustomed to strange faces, and this fact in turn affected the faces and manners of the natives, who became more citified than the population figures might seem to have warranted. In the downtown district Fort Penn had a more or less calculable number of out-of-towners who would be likely to transact business and do their shopping in a city of 80,000; to this number were added the large number of persons who had come to town on state or county matters. The state and county buildings were tax-free and added nothing to the public income of Fort Penn, but land in proximity to the governmental centers was more valuable, hence the downtown district was assessed more highly than in other cities of similar ranking in the national population figures, and consequently the buildings were taller in Fort Penn than they might have been if the city had not been the capital and county seat.

O'Hara's graphic manner of "reportage" on these same realities receives added emphasis in the form of social reference here:

> The Northend Park development . . . had a nice standing in Fort Penn. When a young woman gave her address as Washington, Adams, Jefferson, or Garfield Terrace, or Massachusetts, Ohio, or Florida Drive, the person waiting on her in a Fort Penn department store would look up and smile and say, "That's Northend Park, isn't it?" and whether the clerk said so or not the young colonist would know that the clerk was hoping some day to live there. It was a synonym and a symbol of young, white-collar, Gentile, at least second-generation Fort Penn, most of whom could be sure of small legacies in the not too remote future, and the young colonist would not have to wait while her charge account was being verified. The earlier houses were modified California bungalows, the second batch were Cape Cod cottages, modified to allow for the porch.

Fort Penn has a history of its own. John O'Hara not only gives us the sociology of Nesquehela County in *A Rage to Live;* there are passages which provide portraiture of life in Fort Penn on both of two levels. One is that of locale. The other involves local history as manifested against the backdrop of national events. Thus (in regard to the former), the following passages illustrate Fort Penn's development through time. The marriage of Sidney Tate to Grace Caldwell is such an event:

> The wedding was conceded to be the biggest thing of its kind ever held in Fort Penn. Everybody agreed on that, from the very small group who actually witnessed the ceremony to the thousands who knew all about it. Like everything the Caldwells did, it had to be unique. Grace's wedding started being unique with the invitations: the important weddings in Fort Penn always had followed the "system of taking care of the sheep and the goats by inviting the persons of goat status to the church but not to the reception."

Once more, as previously in *Appointment in Samarra,* O'Hara's examinations into genealogy appear in such a passage as the one following:

> "Ah, yes. I see what you mean. I say amalgamate, and you get my meaning. You say genealogy, and I get your meaning," said the citizen. "If you're inquiring about Mayflower passengers, colonial governors—no. I'm under the impression that there was a Caldwell connection in the House of Burgesses, but the connection isn't very close. Collateral, I guess."

On page 500, O'Hara minutely qualifies the particulars of local history:

> At the time the Caldwell house was built, Second Street actually was the river-front street. The larger houses on Front Street came later, shutting off the Second Streeters' view of the river, but providing the growing city with substantial new revenues from the re-assessed properties, as well as more imposing residences than the large but undeniably staid homes. Values increased rather than decreased, because, it was said, old families like the Caldwells and the Schoffstalls stubbornly refused to move to Front Street, and Second Street thus held its prestige.

Family relationships receive throughout *A Rage to Live* a most minute and at times, staggering amount of attention:

"Thank you," said the citizen. "Well, what I was aiming at is, the Will Caldwells are probably not the richest people in Fort Penn, and I've heard it said they never were the richest, but you can safely say that Grace's family have been among the richest longer than any family in Fort Penn."

"But they're not the richest?"

"No. I could name two or three families today I think have more money. The Isaac Schoffstalls, and some say coony old Andrew O'Brien, that owns the Boston Store. And Fred Bauer's often mention, and I've heard it said Miles Brinkerhoff has more than you think. Miles has the bakery, but he's also in with a powder mill that cleaned up in '98, and I understand he got one of the country banks when the local light company was . . . amalgamated, if you know what I mean."

At other times, O'Hara writes of how people in Fort Penn respond to events of national significance. A particular vignette in the first part of *A Rage to Live* is of curious interest for its illustrating New Year's Eve, 1899-1900 at the Caldwell home. Speaking is Grace Caldwell's father, William:

I don't think Bryan can cause any serious trouble in our country. I hope not. And you young people have no idea how much it's going to mean to the United States, this . . . new Open Door policy in the Far East. Untold wealth. Untold. Wealth beyond the dreams of avarice. And here at home. Think of what they'll be able to do with electricity. In a few years, I don't think we'll use gas for anything but cooking, and I must say I welcome that. The X-Ray, they're working on that all the time, so that it won't be long before the doctors won't have to cut you open to see what's the matter with you.

There we are.

. . . there go the whistles. Five minutes left of good old nineteenth century. Five minutes, the old century ticking away. Just a few minutes before Nineteen Hundred. Come here, my dear, and hold my hand, the last few minutes of the century that brought us together, and all your fathers and mothers together. Boys and girls, I drink to you, the hope of the 1900's, and to our friends, your fathers and mothers.

O'Hara reveals life in Nesquehela during the years 1914-18 by taking ordinary people and, while never commenting on the events which affect them, revealing their reactions. Roger Bannon, who is later to become Grace Tate's lover, decides to form an Irish company to enter the war. Sidney Tate's friend Paul Reichelderfer takes a sporting interest in the conflict, commenting that "If Germans were fighting . . . Italians, I'd be for the Germans, maybe about as strongly as I am for Yale against Harvard." Sidney Tate's moment of disappointment occurs after being rejected by the Navy for physical reasons. A few days later he dies of infantile paralysis. His wife Grace, in keeping with her station, does charity work for the Red Cross.

Any number of critics (Harvey Breit,[27] Lee Rogow,[28] and John Woodburn,[29] particularly) have criticized *A Rage to Live* on the basis of O'Hara's inability to create an important and complex leading character. Much of this criticism would either imply or maintain outright that neither Grace nor Sidney Tate undergoes any appreciable change in character. According to John Woodburn:

> The astonishing thing about *A Rage to Live* is that O'Hara who has almost always written with such insight that I had begun to think no one was safe from him, could do such a thin job on his heroine. She is neither wholly understood nor satisfactorily explained.[30]

This conception of the heroine, however, exists to reveal her consistently and predictably at the mercy of her whims. If as nothing else, Grace is revealed as a wanton. Her character is constant, as is that of her husband, Sidney. Every phase of her life, even during childhood, shows her as being unchangeably under the influence of the principle of sexual pleasure. While the critics cited above may not be in error with regard to any *other* of Grace's character components, O'Hara insists at all times upon sensuality as Grace's distinguishing characteristic. It is neither by mistake, nor for the purpose of sensationalism that the author so graphically describes the boudoir aspects of Grace Tate's love life, or, for that matter, even as they take place in the most unromantic circumstances possible. One of these is Grace's final speech to Ned Minor, a character pursuing an intimate relationship with Grace. Minor appears only once at the very end of the novel, and then only in a telephone conversation with Grace—yet even here O'Hara uses this minute episode to point up Grace's unswerving libidinalism.

But O'Hara uses Grace Tate's unheroic nature not in order to make of her a principal character, or even to make of her static conceptualization a thing of value in its own right. Against the theme of Grace's sensuality, O'Hara plays the counter-theme of her husband's essentially moral nature. One of the two main sources of interest in *A Rage to Live* resides in this opposition of these two temperaments. There is as much substance to Sidney Tate's unchanging characterization as a man of principle as in Grace's as a woman bent only on satisfying her pleasurable urges.

The portrayal of Sidney Tate is the only specifically moral element in this novel. Otherwise the quality of *A Rage to Live,* emphasizing locale and setting as the two other novels do not, is that of a "notebook" novelist.

Together, the two major characters must clash and conflict. The secondary motif of the novel is its moral intent. The primary motif is to reveal graphically life in the raw throughout every stratum of Nesquehela County. There is little complexity in the characters of Grace Tate and her husband; the relationship they create rather than their individual intricacies of character, makes up the tragedy of *A Rage to Live.* The death of Sidney Tate is only an unfortunate postlude to the tragedy.[31] This even Harvey Breit will concede; not only that Sidney Tate is the novel's most admirable character, but that

> The break between husband and wife is one of the best things Mr. O'Hara has ever done. . . . It [the break] is powerful and absolutely right. . . . It ensnares the reader, making him desperately wish that things might be better than they are, and making him desperately know that this is the way the world ends (not with a bang, and *not* with a whimper), quietly, perhaps desperately, but in a principled stand.[32]

Sidney Tate dies after breaking with his wife. Grace suffers the death of her young son and conducts her affairs in an even more responsible fashion. Plot (in the matter of defection between the married couple) and setting (involving O'Hara's exhaustive and graphic representation of the details of Pennsylvania country life) are thus the two dominant and contending thematic elements of *A Rage to Live*.

Ten North Frederick combines the moral despair of life among the Gibbsville upper middle class, as does *Appointment in Samarra*, with the sheer descriptive volume of *A Rage to Live*. In *Ten North Frederick*, O'Hara means to flagellate the pettiness and hypocrisy of Joe Chapin's peers as well as to include a panoramic system of mimetic details of life on every social and occupational level in Gibbsville. *Ten North Frederick* is the work of a moralist who is also a "notebook" novelist.

O'Hara sharpens his focus in *Ten North Frederick* upon the superfices of class snobbery. This time, being from Gibbsville is emphasized as a mark of social disfavor—and O'Hara underscores with more force than previously the inherent iniquity and moral degeneracy of the "Second Thursdays' Club" and Lantenengo society. In *Ten North Frederick*, O'Hara morally judges these realities as well as represents them in a fictional medium.

O'Hara presents Joe Chapin as prosperous, affluent, decorous and discreet. But O'Hara also gives us Joe Chapin, unsuccessful politically though successful in business. Chapin is the ideal family man, but is also the frustrated lover in an affair outside his marriage. He is a remote husband and disappointed father. So it is with most of the people here. Their "good" side, as the outer world sees it, is shown—but so is their "bad" side, as the outer world either never sees it or will not allow itself to see it. Edith Chapin, who "dressed like a member, belonging exactly to her class" is also shown to be pathological and perverted sexually. The Chapins' children, Ann and Joby, suffer likewise. Ann, always having desired love from her remote father, immediately marries, on slight provocation, an Italian musician. Joby, while talented as a jazz pianist ". . . is no damn good. . . . We get a lot of funny reports on him." Or, so say two of Joe's contemporaries. As Robert Gorham Davis notes, "The mistake a couple can make is to let the outside world inside for a brief second's look at a brief second of unhappiness. Then the unity is broken." [33]

Ten North Frederick aims to provide that look at this couple's unhappiness, but it is a look that lasts not a brief second but for nearly three whole generations of unhappiness in the lives of the couple, their parents and their children. Nor are any of the characters outside the Chapin family, however "minor" they may be as characters—free from this vision. O'Hara depicts, for example, even the only occasionally or once mentioned character if only by letting us hear him talk. Mike Slattery, for example, who is responsible for Joe's ultimate political defeat, is shown as a Machiavellian local boss. His defeat of Joe Chapin is also revealed as the outcome merely of a personal quarrel. There is a parallel to Slattery in the figure of Conrad Yates, a vulgar and politically ambitious mayor of Gibbsville. Arthur McHenry, Joe's law partner and best friend, O'Hara presents as the one person who has known Joe beneath his facade.

The one passage in *Ten North Frederick* most relevant to the manner of life which most of its characters (at least those from its upper ranges of social strata) must endure occurs early in the novel, after the death of Joe Chapin. Says an attorney to Chapin's business partner, Arthur McHenry, during a social conversation: "The safest way to live is first, inherit money. Second, marry a woman that will co-operate with you in your sexual peculiarities. Third, have a legitimate job that keeps you busy. Fourth, be born without a taste for liquor. Fifth, join some big church. Sixth, don't live too long."

The people O'Hara displays so tellingly in terms of their intimate personal lives are at the mercy either of the impersonal, historic effect of life in American society, or of their glands. They are none of them responsible for their actions, being held in check by forces beyond themselves. "The social forces their acts release seem to have an independent being apart from the people they destroy." Joe Chapin can never become President both because of his difference with Mike Slattery, local Republican opportunist, and because, ultimately, of his apparently high, but actually limited, social station. Joe's wife, Edith, has had a Lesbian affair as a young girl. This is why her married life must remain a tragedy. These are only two examples of people in *Ten North Frederick* who cannot call their lives their own. Robert Gorham Davis remarks appropriately that "The principal characters in these novels are not worse than other people; in some ways they are better. But they are unlucky."

It has always been John O'Hara's purpose to let the reader know "this is what happened"—and also, to let him know "this is how it happened." Yet neither of these realities constitutes what any of us who are not thoroughgoing masochists would desire, or even admit, is the natural course of events in life. This includes the death of Joe Chapin, one of the book's few admirable figures. It includes, on the more general level, the depiction of a whole community founded upon fraud, deceit, pettiness, and bigotry—the life of the Gibbsville Club, the Gibbsville Assembly, the Second Thursdays. "How it happened" is no more pleasant. Joe Chapin dies of the physical effects brought on by an emotional upheaval. His marriage to Edith Stokes is in turn ruined by her sexual inadequacy—and this union of the two parents can result only in unhappy lives for Joby and Ann Chapin. Whether one agrees with the view of cosmic despair expressed in *Ten North Frederick* or not, he nevertheless tends to feel it more strongly with each reading of the book. "You have the sensation," St. Clair McKelway has said justly, "of being not in the middle of a book but in the middle of life." [34] And, in the midst of *such* a life, one can only prepare for death.

O'Hara shows Gibbsville society in its formal as well as informal moments. In the following passage O'Hara stresses the vicious decadence of the Chapins' fellow Gibbsvillians:

There were the inevitable few of whom Arthur or Edith would say: "We'll send him an invitation, but he'll have sense enough not to come." . . . Two special policemen from a detective agency were hired to keep out the uninvited, a precaution ironically required by the fact that liquor would be served in violation of the

national and club rules. . . . All agreed that it has been a splen-
did party, over and above such misfortunes as a lady's lost ear-
ring, the early departure of several of the elderly, a man who had
lost the keys to his car, another man who had chucked [in] the
bathroom . . . and in addition to the misfortunes that were dis-
cussed at the supper party there were a few others . . . and the
small incident [of Jane Weeks and her dinner partner] in which
Jane said, "Are you by chance a customer of my husband's firm?"
"No," said the man.
"Then take your hand off my leg."

The opening chapters of *Ten North Frederick*—those
devoted to Joe Chapin's funeral—immediately point to Edith
Chapin, Joe's wife, as a prime cause of Joe's death through alcoholism.

[Edith Chapin] in action was a lesson in graciousness under
difficult conditions. For each group she had one special thing to
say, a general comment or observation that would reach every
man and woman in the group. In one group it would be the
weather: the snow had not fallen. In another, the text of the clergyman's words; in another, the flowers . . . in another, the per-
ennial beauty of old Trinity itself; in another, how much Joe
would have enjoyed it all. Each group was created, and skillfully.

Also, just after the funeral,

. . . Friends were beginning to bore you as much as enemies, and
the ones quickly became the other over nothing more important
than a near-sighted revoke at bridge. But a gathering of this kind
briefly took on a party atmosphere because there were so many
like you present. No matter how truly you believed that you
wanted to be alone, a gathering of this kind did stave off loneli-
ness. . . . The party arrivals accepted their drinks and sat down
to rest, staying out of the dining room to make polite, irrelevant
conversation, and greeting each other (whom they had last seen
less than thirty minutes ago at the graveside) with a reunion
heartiness, nicely modulated.

Being from Gibbsville is thus revealed as being at a social disadvantage. Joe Chapin's later years only point up the
barriers to his political ambition to become President, deter-
rents which have their origins in Joe's unappealing place of

birth and upbringing. Social class is a determinant in the life of Joe Chapin; it prevents him from being able to live away from the restrictions of his milieu. For such a reason, he cannot marry the woman of his choice. Besides, Joe Chapin cannot scale the social ladder to a sufficiently high rung in order to enable him to overcome the "disgrace" of his beginnings.

> . . . On Joe's income [his family] could have travelled to the far places and seen the strange things, the lands and people that they knew through Stoddard's Lectures. But who in Shanghai, China, would know that in Gibbsville, Pennsylvania, U.S.A., Joseph B. Chapin was an aristocrat of unassailable standing? If a Chinese prince were to come to Gibbsville, he would be entertained by the Chapins, but if the Chapins were visiting in Pekin, would the reverse be true? Closer to home, to take up residence in Philadelphia or New York was not a prospect that attracted Edith. It would require much, much greater wealth than Joe possessed to get established in the big American cities. Joe could, of course, continue his legal career, but that was not to live as a retired gentleman.

Sex is still another determinant in the lives of all major characters in *Ten North Frederick*. In the three Gibbsville novels, sex is more than either diversion, or as many critics (among them *Time Magazine's*,[35] and Leslie Fiedler [36]) claim, sheer titillation. Sex affects the lives of all the Chapins and those around them. None of these people can perform a sexual act, no matter now privately—without their being affected by it in later life. In a writer such as F. Scott Fitzgerald or Ernest Hemingway, love-making might be carried on with a complete disregard for the consequences. Amory Blaine or Lieutenant Henry might "have" a woman whenever he chose. His *anticipation* of the climax would be as important as the ultimate sexual delight itself. This is not the case with Joe Chapin, who drinks himself into an early grave after suffering from the remorse of not being able ever to marry a classmate's daughter with whom he has had an affair. Nor is this the case with Edith Chapin, whose homosexual attachment in boarding-school ultimately causes the ruin of her marriage to Joe and also chronically affects the lives of their children. All these people are acted upon by sex—and they live their sex lives with no sense of possible doom for themselves or for others in their behavior. The Chapins' daughter, Ann, affords still another example. She is started upon her "downward path" after an affair with Charley Bongiorno, a jazz musician. After a brief marriage to Bongiorno, she then has an abortion and the marriage is annulled. Ann arrives at a state of nymphomania after a multitude of affairs, such as the one in which she awakes in a man's deserted apartment.

> In her first year in New York, Ann had slept with four, and possibly five—she was not sure—men. . . . One morning she awoke in a man's apartment, nude, and in the single large bed, with no idea of the man's name or what he looked like. . . . She searched for a picture that might recall what he looked like, and on a sudden inspiration she looked up the name in a college yearbook in his bookshelf. His name was there, and a distinct photograph, but she remembered nothing about him.

Edith Chapin "did love Joe, as an adjunct, as a part of herself and a mechanism in her life." But, she never appreciates Joe in such a manner that she can give of herself, or in any way assume a passive role either sexually or as a marriage partner. Basically, Edith hates men. She will not admit defeat by allowing herself to be ruled by a man. After their first wedding experience Edith announces to Joe, who is fast asleep:

> "I own you," she said. "At last." . . . And she began to understand that he was going to take a lot of owning and that she had been wrong in thinking that owning him was going to be so quick and simple a matter as she had hoped and believed. . . . It was not love; love might easily have very little to do with it; but it was as strong a desire as love or hate and it was going to be her life, the owning of this man.

Later in the novel, Edith meets "Barbara Danworth . . . a passionate and passionately devoted little thing who must now be thirty-nine." Barbara says to Edith, "Now don't be haughty, Edith. Don't be one hundred per cent American. Remember, you started me, 'way back at Hannah Payne's School, and you'd never been anywhere but Gibbsville, Pennsylvania." Thus,

Edith's Lesbianism comes full cycle, as does much of the sexual activity in this novel. After this reencounter, the author remarks:

> . . . If the Deity wanted to mete out an elaborate and belated punishment, that was the way He would do it. . . . An outburst of revelation was something she had avoided all her life, simply because utter frankness was not in her nature. *Why* it was not in her nature was not a secret she kept from herself; she gave only what she had to give, to get more in return.

Edith also seeks to release the pent-up passion which never finds an outlet in her relations with Joe. She does this by having an affair with Lloyd Williams, who later in the book becomes District Attorney. She rationalizes that "I'm very grateful . . . for the love-making. I quarreled with my husband. Now I'll go back to him without carrying over any resentment and he'll think I'm a dear and gentle wife." But, by the time Williams has advanced, politically, Edith is at the mercy of Williams.

> . . . Now, if she were to use him and he were to brag about it, now that he was the District Attorney and on his way up, he could blab it in any saloon in the country and be believed and remain unharmed.

Joe Chapin, however, is the most powerfully affected character, in respect to the "boomerang" effect of his own grand passion. Within ten years of his death, Joe has an affair with his daughter's New York roommate, Kate Drummond. It is probably the only "affair" in his entire life, and certainly the only meaningful love relationship.

Until meeting Kate, and even all through his married life, Joe Chapin is the model of restraint, of upper-middleclass decorum. Joe and Edith Chapin "were living in a time when it was popularly remarked that 'he never looked at another woman.' Joe did look at other women, handsomer women—but never strayed from his wife. He was a gentleman." It is also not until meeting Kate that Joe realizes the failure of his marriage to Edith, and shortly thereafter he has his affair with Kate.

But now, this relationship is doomed. Kate says:

. . . my marrying you would be just as bad as your making me your mistress. It would do almost the same things to your life. Cutting you off from your friends. You'd be embarrassed when you saw my father. You'd worry about what Ann was thinking. You'd be conscious of the differences in age between you and my friends. Even now, on account of Ann, I can't quite make myself call you Joe.

The relationship is destined to suffer because, ironically enough, of the social pressures involved.

Joe Chapin's death through alcoholism is on its way. The "determinism" of sex has come full cycle. Joe becomes a steady drinker through the remorse brought about in his life by Kate. He finally dies of cirrhosis of the liver. Joe tells his feelings to Kate just once:

. . . everything the same as when I left there yesterday morning. But I won't be the same. Practically nobody in town will know I've been away, and won't know I've come back to what? To nothing, to everything that's away from you, Kate. To nothing. To death. To the end of life. To death. To life away from you.

He last sees Kate at a restaurant for lunch, and as they are about to leave, says to her, "The waiter now thinks that the middle-aged gentleman has persuaded the beautiful, young lady—well, we know what he thinks." Then,

As the years went by, and beginning rather soon after Joe's hotel luncheon with Kate Drummond, the silences were longer, and whiskey became a part of the meetings [between Joe and Arthur McHenry] . . . Joe, after his last lunch with Kate, stopped putting ice in his drinks and the proportion of water to whiskey became closer to even. The quiet drinking never increased to the point where Arthur, saying good night, could have called his friend drunk, but he could not help noticing that every night there was a fresh, new bottle, and without asking, Arthur had no way of knowing how long Joe would sit in the den, smoking a pipe, humming old songs, sipping watered whiskey and reviewing his life.

Such "was Joe's life during the final unresponding years."

Ten North Frederick is, finally, an objectification of John O'Hara's essential pessimism towards life in general. Just as *Appointment in Samarra* is an example of O'Hara's social snobbery, and *A Rage to Live* an illustration of his command of graphic genre—so *Ten North Frederick* embodies these things but goes beyond them in an underlying morbidity and the sense of a hostile universe. Although one may see in Joe Chapin and his family much of social importance, as members of Gibbsville's "first family," there is, this time, an emphasis upon their essentially unhappy side. In *A Rage to Live*, O'Hara makes of the death of Sidney Caldwell a domestic tragedy. But in *Ten North Frederick*, Joe Chapin, also *pater-familias* and principal male character, exemplifies *life* as being even more tragic. Says Robert Gorham Davis: "In *Ten North Frederick* life is the tragedy, as before, and O'Hara, while making use of death, has managed to let even his climax grow out of life." [37]

From the Terrace moves on a mechanism of coincidence like none of the novels preceding itself. There is an incidence of death by violent and totally unforeseeable circumstance that overwhelms the reader by means of its at times close to absurd naivete on the part of O'Hara that assumes so casual an intervention by mortal tragedy in the lives of all the personages. Not since the career of Harry Morgan has so fortuitous a series of chaotic mishaps been the lot of any protagonist (as well as any number of the novel's minor characters) as in the case of Alfred Eaton. True, these drastic experiences, taken in sum total or individually by Eaton, possess an indelible effect upon the creation of Eaton's conscience throughout his entire life. This is the primary defense implicit in the gradual revelation of Eaton's moral severity toward himself and others as well. However, there will exist considerable doubt in the minds of many readers as to the validity of O'Hara's excessive and at times depressive and even boring proliferation of the text by each violent episode following so. closely upon the one before. As *From the Terrace* is O'Hara's longest novel (897 pages), the reading and enjoyment of such a work is often intruded upon by the time one must often exert in order to wonder whether

O'Hara could have done as effective a characterization of Alfred Eaton as the novel's significant agent of moral outcry, simply by using fewer examples with greater economy and compactness than is the case. Sidney Tate dies prematurely in *A Rage to Live*. This is, nevertheless, O'Hara's only previous usage of such coincidence—and even then it exists mainly for the purpose of demonstrating Grace Tate's impiety in the face of such an event. *From the Terrace,* while in many other respects an excellent novel, suffers from the incongruity of such repetitive and untoward mishaps that exist in the midst of so graphically descriptive a narrative of the *modus vivendi* particular to Port Johnson, Pennsylvania.

The initial cataclysm for Alfred Eaton occurs at age eleven. His brother dies of spinal meningitis. Alfred has always been aware of the enmity of his father, which becomes for Alfred only too manifest at this point. It is not enough that all along Alfred Eaton has been thus aware of his intrusion upon his brother's sanctity. At the younger brother's death, Eaton

> . . . was living without a philosophy, but he had learned that his father did not love him and did love Billy, and his father's love was just something he could not have. . . . He could live without his father's love, because he had to. . . . But [this] knowledge did not keep him from wondering what you did to make your father love you.

From this point on, Eaton's moral consciousness becomes his dominating passion. The emotional conflict growing out of this occurs for Eaton even later, during his forties. It is his "private hell." Eaton exclaims, ". . . People . . . think and behave as individuals first, and as units of a family second—and a bad second. . . . There is no *natural* law that says brother has to love brother. . . ."

When Eaton reaches eighteen, there occurs the death of Victoria Dockwiler, a girl he has known from childhood. At a dance, Eaton is aware of a rival, Peter Van Peltz. He challenges Van Peltz to a fight and is refused when Victoria rejects him on the spot. The two others drive off and are killed in an accident that evening. Shortly after this, while at college, Eaton is temporarily kidnapped by some upperclassmen who leave him on a country road until close to death by exposure. However, the humiliation and the physical suffering Eaton undergoes are of little anguish to him, as the guilt perceived at his desire (however natural) to punish his aggressors. This is equally the case when later that year Eaton goes out of his way to visit a man in Philadelphia named Frolick. It is made apparent that Alfred Eaton's mother has committed adultery with Frolick. Eaton pommels him into submission but cannot afterward admit to himself that only the trait of his own possessiveness has made him behave so reprisefully.

> And throughout all phases of his self-blame—his guilt in the Frolick episode; his desire for revenge in the Hopewell incident; his clear responsibility for what had happened to Victoria and Peter —he had an expectation of punishment that was so strong as to be a need; . . . Hence his fear, . . . and his terror, made worse by his inability to release some of it in an expression of his guilt and alarm to another person.

Norma Budd is a woman seven years older than Eaton. She is the partner in his first affair, an event of such significance to him that although Eaton believes himself to be in love, he cannot accustom himself to her superior knowledge in two areas. These are her sophistication in the physical phase of their relationship, but more important than this, her mature awareness of the total inadvisability of extending the liaison beyond the confines of sensual indulgence, however it may be tempered by mutual respect. In a moment of suppressed resentment, Eaton stalks out of her apartment. Shortly thereafter, Norma Budd dies at the hands of another lover. Eaton's natural reaction, by now, is to feel nothing less than direct responsibility.

> . . . The two girls to whom he had meant something, who had meant the most to him, had been killed; one in an accident that occurred only minutes away from his actual presence and in which he could soberly and without melodrama admit to having had an influencing part. It was hard to relate Norma's murder to himself, but for that reason, just as hard to claim total innocence. In the one case he had been quite directly responsible; in the other, his

responsibility was indirect and remote, but spiritually real. And if he had wanted to, he could not deny that he had been unlucky for the two girls he had loved, the only two. . . . He could see that in failing Norma he had made it possible for her to become more deeply involved with Waterford, with the final, inevitable result. . . .

At the beginning of the First World War, Eaton receives a Naval commission. After returning to civilian life, he refuses his father's offer of a share in the family steel mill. Typical of Samuel Eaton's reaction to his son's demur is the proviso that, in his own words,

"I was hoping we'd be friends, but first you were going to have to show me you were the kind of man I'd *want* to be friends with. The job in the mill was going to be yours, and I hoped the friendship would grow out of that."

Eaton marries Mary St. John shortly after this talk with his father. Days before the wedding, Samuel Eaton dies. It is as if he might have said to his son, ". . . 'I will not even be alive on your big day.' . . . [Alfred] never doubted that his father had died deliberately."

Eaton forms a partnership with his friend, Alex Porter. It is the Nassau Aeronautical Corporation. Later he withdraws and the venture, like his marriage, fails. He obtains another position, this time with James D. MacHardie, a New York investigating executive.

It is by an equally close to impossible happenstance which next affects the destiny of Eaton. He saves a drowning child after it has fallen into an ice-covered pond. The boy turns out to be none other than the grandson of James D. MacHardie, who offers Eaton immediate employment in his firm. MacHardie asks him what course he would follow, assuming that he owned a million dollars. Eaton's answer: "Today? I'd wait until you offered me a job, and then I'd take it." The next bizarre coincidence involves Eaton's meeting with Natalie Benziger, his second wife. This becomes all the more possible when Natalie's husband, Ben Eustace, very conveniently dies at the height of their romance. There has developed meanwhile the tragedy of Eaton's son, Rowland, killed while in service. *From the Terrace* next has only to portray the degeneration of Alfred Eaton into a caricature of his better potential, or the re-personalization of "Archy Busby."

For all the contrivedness of its plot-outline, *From the Terrace* offers just by such means its most appreciable thematic divergence from any of the novels preceding itself. Consider this in the light of O'Hara's previous remark in *Ten North Frederick*. Here he remarks that

> . . . there are few occurrences—if there are any—that bring about radical and quick changes in the lives of human beings. Change is always fluid; rapidly fluid or slowly fluid; but even major events in a human life do not make the overnight personality changes that they are said to make. . . . [They] all take time, to be absorbed by the soul. . . .

From the Terrace, on the other hand, allows an entire profusion of such events to occur in such a fashion as to affect all its major characters in an equally indeterminate and rash fashion. That "change *is* sudden" is now the crux of O'Hara's attitude toward his fictional material. All along, it has been just the contrary—that change never is and never can be sudden. Neither is the change in the psyche of each of the people described in this novel free from such instantaneous alteration. In spite of the dubious character of the verisimilitude of most of the important objective causes and emotional effects, *From the Terrace* manages to demonstrate the plausibility of its premise that in spite of their material advantages, the persons in Alfred Eaton's coterie are as subject to the unpredictability of their fate as anyone else. Their capacity for happiness or despair is in no wise affected.

Alfred Eaton's father-in-law, Eugene St. John, describes this to him in the novel's most outspoken declaration of its own theory of causality:

> . . . something absolutely unpredictable happens, and automatically your life is changed for you. In a few hours' time you change from an irresponsible young man to the active head of a family, and that removes a lot of the objections we had to you as a pro-

spective son-in-law. Life is full of these ironies. A man that you don't like very much has an unfortunate accident, and through it you get what you want. [*Vide* Ben Eustace] . . . Do you see how all these things are interrelated and yet completely unpredictable? . . .

Eaton's rejoinder contains within its own saying the body of the novel's fatalism up to that point in his own life, and long afterward.

> "It goes back to a fight I was in at Princeton. That's how I got to be friends with Lex Porter, and through him, met Mary. Or, if my father hadn't given me a new car I might not have driven to Long Island that night. If I hadn't had the car, I wouldn't have taken the train. So there's my father again. Or, if it hadn't been for an automobile accident at home, I'd probably have had a Stutz instead of a Marmon, and maybe the man that drove a new Stutz from Indiana wouldn't have arrived the same day that the man did with the Marmon, and I wouldn't have met Mary. And if I hadn't been so—" He stopped himself: he was thinking of his quarrel with Victoria Dockwiler and her ride in the Stutz. "Too many if's."

We then have the condemnation of Alfred Eaton to the perpetual punishment raised by his own conscience. Eaton is endowed with money, the power to spend it in such a manner as to affect the lives of countless others, and the social prestige to enable him to do so with sufficient impunity. However, his regard for moral compunction is the factor in keeping him from attaining the complete admiration of his contemporaries and in being adequately able to respect himself to the extent of avoiding the revivification in his own person as "Archy Busby." His life, as it occurs within the pages of *From the Terrace,* displays his earlier life as the period of incubation for his overtly rigorous moral self-flagellation. This is succeeded by the years with MacHardie as the attempt to overcome the sense of Eaton's moral atrophy developed during the years of childhood and youth.

The ultimate pathos in the life of Alfred Eaton is the "Archy Busby," or final stage of his life. The man so named is a former Wall Street bond salesman who ended his life a suicide.

He is "A symbol. He was a real person. But he's a symbol of all the Yale guys and Princeton guys and Jekyll Island and Links Club nice guys that for some reason didn't quite make it. Forty. Forty-five. Fifty. . . . But they're always around, professional Yale men or Princeton men. Reunions. Games. Professional uncles, too. . . ." Paradoxically enough, Eaton's reduction to such purely decorative status is the result of his own moral hypersensitivity. Not only does he isolate himself from the company of most of his business associates—Rothermel, Jack Tom Smith, Creighton Duffy and Lawrence Von Elm. This in turn derives from his perennially vindictive and at times exacerbative moral scorn that he has turned upon them preceding the period as "Archy Busby." This eclipsular phase begins at the time Eaton has left his position as Assistant Secretary of the Navy and is in search of employment. There has taken place a falling-out with Jack Tom Smith, a Texas oil millionaire. "*They* don't call it loafing, *or* looking around. They call it out-of-a-job. . . ." Because of his own self-despisal, Eaton loses no time in affirming this attitude in the form of its being taken out on others. He thus finds compensation for this in being able to prove to himself that even worse examples of moral ineptitude than his own must exist in others. By the end of *From the Terrace*, the mechanism of reprisal against Eaton's tendency to censorial opprobrium has come full cycle. Alfred Eaton is finally hoisted up by the petard of his own self-negation which is so actively if unknowingly applied to others.

Eaton, in spite of all his moral severity, possesses a sensual side to his character. He is the personification of John O'Hara's reference to himself as a "common ordinary guy who likes common ordinary things," while at the same time more than so commonly aware of the value of social discretion. The sole redeeming object in the otherwise tragic depiction of Alfred Eaton is the at any rate temporary happiness of his marriage to Natalie Benziger. Nevertheless, Eaton's single moment of redemption from the accumulated sorrows of his life up until his second marriage, consists of this relationship. But even this cannot endure. In the end, Natalie must accustom herself to accepting the lot of wife to a man fallen to this low state of grace. The most poignant, if pathetic awareness of Eaton's tragedy of character occurs as Natalie overhears the telephone conversation which closes the novel and with itself, Natalie's respect for the man who might have remained her husband and lover:

> Natalie listened to his words, and easily supplied most of Shanley's words she could not hear. It had come, it was here, as she had seen it coming, and the only real surprise was in discovering that in pitying Alfred she could hate him. Not for his weakness— the pity was for that. But for counting on her love to make him believe that his weakness was strength.

From the Terrace is no less a disquisition (and a stricture) upon the evils of social class distinction than any of John O'Hara's other "Lantenengo" novels. Yet here too another thematic difference arises, until now fully unexploited. Alfred Eaton is the product of money long accumulated and spent as freely in the interests of others as in those of oneself. His attitude toward his social stratum is one of resignation rather than pursuit. Even on those rare occasions of encounter with a person of greater means than himself, Eaton remains calm, never envious or self-demeaning. For him to climb any higher on the upperclass ladder of success could only be regarded as redundance for its own sake. Alfred Eaton is a man of principles, aware of the obligations toward individuals deriving from lower echelons than his own. He is never shown as a "climber"—only as a stationary agent.

This is not the case, as regards Eaton's foremost enemies. All of them strive for some means of asserting their own social equality with Eaton. It is, however, to their greatest moral discredit that they refuse to accept the inevitability of their arrangement in the pattern of class gradation. In their striving for increasingly honorific social station, they become objects of derision rather than pathos. That they cannot, like the father of Natalie Benziger, leave well enough alone in consignment only to the lower or median levels in the upperclass milieu is, for O'Hara, the nature of their amorality. Moreover, they even may decry the plenitude surrounding the lives of The Very

Rich, only to revel gracelessly and selfishly in the luxury and privilege which becomes their lot as soon as they become materially able to attain such station themselves. O'Hara, in outlining the lives of such persons as Rothermel, Roper, Jack Tom Smith, or Lawrence Von Elm, from their earliest appearance renders it apparent that it is envy rather than altruistic concern for issues of economic inequity, which motivates them to antipathy for Alfred Eaton.

Two such examples, among several others, are provided by Tom Rothermel and Jim Roper. Rothermel grows up in Port Johnson contemporaneously with Eaton. "Money . . . was not a lively topic of concern in the . . . Eaton family; as a topic it was considered to be in bad taste. At Jonas Rothermel's house it was unifying, like a common friend and a common enemy, an ambition and an elusive gain." By contrast, in the Eaton household, the discussion of money is discouraged by a ". . . rule created by taste, like the rule that a boy did not wear one brown shoe and one black shoe, that a young girl did not wear jewelry, that the things you ate with a fork you did not eat with a spoon. . . ." As Tom Rothermel progresses in age, his parents put aside money to finance his education at Penn State. Rothermel later finds it necessary to request a loan from Eaton. There is never any mention made of Rothermel's repayment of the money.

In the characterization of Tom Rothermel, O'Hara creates a caricature of the middleclass Marxist that is easily the equivalent to any of these similar stereotypes in Joseph Conrad's *The Secret Agent*. Rothermel grows up adhering to the standards of his lower-middleclass milieu, at the same time declaring the glories of the collectivist state. As the novel proceeds, it becomes increasingly evident that Rothermel will neither alter the *status quo* (so long as it provides him with the instruments of his own vertical mobility), nor will he attempt any show of respect for Eaton, and any other members of the same class, on the grounds of common humanity. ". . . The CP boys would probably call him a deviationist. . . . However, there is little danger that Tom Rothermel will ever be called *Anti*-Communist. Tom is the clean-shaven, Hart, Schafner &

Marx version of the Bolshevik with the bomb and the sparkling fuse in his pocket. . . ." Near the finish of *From the Terrace,* Rothermel is revealed as having said of Eaton, "He's a fascist. . . . A fascist and a labor-busting fink. His latest is to try to take away the working man's ration cards." O'Hara's portraiture of Alfred Eaton as an individual human with a life-history of as considerable and complex an amount of dissatisfaction with his own lot as Rothermel himself, provides the contrast by irony with Rothermel's remark about Eaton. With no regard for either the issue of Eaton's married life and apparent failure as a parent—any more than for Eaton's struggle with his remorseless conscience—Rothermel's pointed remark shows up as evidence of his own moral incipience and not Eaton's.

Jim Roper competes unsuccessfully with Eaton in courting Mary St. John. He gives himself away in admitting to her that ". . . I went to a good school because my father was a clergyman and they gave him a special rate. I had to wait on table in college and miss half the fun because I had to keep up my marks for my scholarship. . . . But it would have been worth it if I could have had you. . . ." It later proves implicit that Roper's only interest lies in his own self-aggrandizement. Because his economic station has been of such median character to prohibit his indulgence in the same way of life as Eaton, Roper attempts through jealousy to obtain the benefits of such exalted social standing without willingness to accept realistically the implausibility of his total success in his social climbing. In short, Roper is an upstart and fortune-hunter. Like Rothermel, he is incapable of any fellow feeling for Alfred Eaton. This is not only because of rivalry. It is because Roper cannot empathize with the qualitative difference in the pressures incumbent upon members of Eaton's "set." Basically, his only capacity for assimilation into such a group is that of envying its ways from an exterior point of observation. His success as regards such acceptance must always remain superficial, not as part of his total pattern of integration. Roper (not completely unlike his very creator at various moments of the latter's development) must always remain in envy of the ways of The Smart Set. It also is interesting to note that Roper, after becoming an M.D.,

later decides to practice as a psychiatrist as part of his medical
career.

From the Terrace is a tragedy of the mundane. Alfred
Eaton is revealed throughout his biography at all phases of age
and conviction, from infancy into his late forties. At the finish,
Eaton regards himself as a parody of what he might have been
in the preceding years. He is now "Archy Busby," or a man
whose only function is to be socially decorative whenever this
becomes the condescending demand by any of his peers. There
would appear to exist no consuming reason for Eaton's descent.
But it is only his own self-condemnation to this ignominy which
constitutes this novel's greatest revelation of character as well as
his reaction to certain mores. In spite of what might appear to
any observer from a lower social stratum as evidence of Eaton's
attainment of a life of grandest munificence, Eaton himself pon-
ders his existence as a thing of failure.

There are two ways to regard this conviction on the part
of Eaton, in From the Terrace. One way is by means of exam-
ining the proof of such an assertion as it appears internally, to
Eaton himself. The other method is to consider Eaton as a victim of surrounding circumstance—much of it occurring in the
form of unpredictable violence. But more important, Eaton
must suffer for the exposure of his qualities of conscience and
honesty in matters relevant to his business and Secretary's position, and in his domestic life besides. The irony implicit in
O'Hara's attitude toward this one central character is such that
whatever qualities of conscience, candor, and honesty with oneself at all times may pervade Eaton's ideals, it is just these same
sterling attributes which contribute to his final debasement.
Alfred Eaton's final degradation is the reversal of that of Frank
Norris' Vandover. It is Eaton's positive adherence to a series of
moral ideals which must constitute his downfall, even though
the nature of those events which act upon him from outside
himself are beyond his control. Vandover, nevertheless, offers
only token resistance to allowing such circumstances to change
his attitude to one of pessimism. Eaton's conscience is his source
of greatest danger. Alfred Eaton becomes a pessimist early in

life and remains one long afterward by seeing, and constantly reasserting to himself, that it is the innocent who must suffer more greatly for their mistakes than the evil ones for their sins.

Ourselves to Know concerns the life of Robert Millhouser up to and briefly after his murder of his wife, Hedda. The murder, however, is merely the culminative event following upon the painstaking effort on the part of the author to reveal gradually the character of Millhouser as being the product of his life situation up until age 53. It is the years afterward which are recorded by Gerald Higgins in this first venture by O'Hara into the Conradian stylism of shifting the narrative from one character to another, beginning in the first person, switching into the third, then back again to the first, until the novel finally finishes in the narrative of Higgins, fifteen years after his last personal encounter with Millhouser. Although any number of critics may find fault with the unwieldiness and somewhat affected use of the split-narrative, there is always a deliberate and never obtrusive sense of direct connection of all the events and subject matter so vividly described by this means of personal shift, with two phases of Millhouser's character. One is Millhouser's attachment, until her death late in his life, to his mother. As a result of this, there occurs the more profound issue of Millhouser's sense of his being emotionally "played out." By the finish of *Ourselves to Know,* the reader is well aware of, if nothing else, the depiction of the character of Robert Millhouser, both as Millhouser himself reveals it to his amanuensis and as Higgins reconstructs the events relevant to Millhouser's perpetual mental "set" in terms of their significance.

Millhouser's life in Lyons, Pa., consists of little more than what is seen of him on his way to social visits in the town and what few business matters he may transact as a trustee of the local bank when not on his farm. Most of his life is spent at home—and after a point it becomes apparent that his "stay-at-home" character may be more than the result of ordinary consanguiniality. There is absolutely no mention made of incest or of abnormal dependency on the part of Millhouser. Never-

theless, the finish of the novel allows the final touch to this
segment of Millhouser's total portraiture. His mother is revealed in Millhouser's own words as someone ". . . who tried
to love me but couldn't. I guess I didn't measure up to my
father or her first husband. . . ." What is most apparent in
Millhouser's life, even until his marriage at 51 to Hedda Steele
who is 18, is the unvarying, not to say depressing, character of
his everyday existence.

> Robert Millhouser attended to his business affairs, he withdrew
> from participation in the social life of Fort Penn, he satisfied his
> sexual needs at a house that was operated by a successor to Mrs.
> Jones, he made no effort to find a successor to [his close friend]
> Dr. Willetts, and while neither he nor [his mother] Zilph Mill-
> houser ever put it into spoken words, they knew that the routine
> into which they settled was to be their mode of life until the
> death of one of the two terminated the routine. . . .

Even the death of his mother ". . . simplified his own life by
taking away the companionship which was a dreary substitute
for the love he had yet to experience." Millhouser is shown
during every phase of his life, even into old age, as a recluse.
His introduction to the upperclass strata of Fort Penn is, by
his own admission, forced upon him. For this reason, he almost
immediately breaks off his engagement to Esther Baumgarten,
to whom he has become introduced. Hereafter, Millhouser's
only contact with women is part of a moneyed proposition.
Millhouser marries Hedda Steele only on the vaguest provocation. In fact, his murder of her in her sleep occurs almost with
no knowledge on the part of Millhouser that he has committed
so extreme and heinous an act. Millhouser is totally devoid of
any reaction to untoward occurrence in reality outside himself
after a trip he has made to Europe with his best friend, Sterling
Calthorp. He believes that he will study painting. His most
overwhelming discovery is that Calthorp is homosexual. The
experience only drives Millhouser further into his own seclu-
sion.

It is during Millhouser's confinement to jail, following
the murder of his wife, that he himself admits his own lack of

emotion as being the substance of his predicament. Not only has his mother's inability to love him in a natural manner been in its own right a source of Millhouser's suffering. It has also made for his empathic decease. ". . . But literally I am insane," Millhouser manages to tell his attorney. "There is something missing, and it's what I've been saving. Feeling, that's what's missing. A normal, sane man would feel remorse for killing a beautiful creature. But I don't feel either remorse or pleasure, the pleasure of revenge. . . ." From this point on, *Ourselves to Know* can be seen as the chronicular description of several events in Millhouser's life in relation to the nature of this emotional mishap. The most astounding thing about *Ourselves to Know* is that so little unusual happens, outside of a murder. If *From the Terrace* is O'Hara's most extravagant novel, in view of its depiction of a way of life so set upon by the forces of extraordinary violence, *Ourselves to Know* is its direct opposite. The chief attribute of *Ourselves to Know* is that it is so capable of revealing to the reader the organic and uninterrupted sense of direct responsibility for each of the actions committed by its protagonist as they are revealed against the more unvarying backdrop of Millhouser's emotional inaccessibility. Whatever one may say about this novel, there is never a sense of the accidental or the superfluous about any of the important events in the text. These would be Millhouser's departure from the friendship of Calthorp, the death of his older comrade, Dr. Willetts, the broken engagement with his fiance, his mother's death and finally the murder of Hedda.

After the death of his mother, Millhouser is presented with little more than the prospect of retreat into his "comfortable monastery." His mother has died, making it even more difficult than before for Millhouser to obtain the closeness which had been his previous demand in living in such close quarters with his mother. It is out of no small desperation that Millhouser immediately seizes upon the opportunity of marriage to Hedda Steele. The physical attraction between the couple serves as the only means of marital promise.

". . . O'Hara projects a bleak and desperate vision of life's emptiness and moral anarchy, redeemed only by the calm courage with which his heroes face their destruction. . . ." This is an excerpt from a review by David Boroff in *Saturday Review*. The transfiguration of Higgins' attitude toward the very material with which he is presented—and especially toward his own sense of the need for change of his own provincialism in matters of moral stringency toward others—is the most outspoken argument for O'Hara's use of the split-consciousness narrative. This latter deploys from Higgins' use of the first-person persona, into the use of Millhouser's own correspondence with him, then into the more objective reconstruction by Higgins of much of Millhouser's career, finally ending in the codification as Higgins relates to the reader that his life has altered in proportion to the intensity of his reaction to the biographic novel which he had originally intended as a Master's thesis. Higgins' development into his moral relativism allows him finally, in the face of his revelation, to accept the unfaithfulness of his mate, Frances, as set forth in the final sentence: ". . . I often tried to think of things like that to take my mind off Frances and the stories that had got back to me." O'Hara's intimation is that Higgins is also not above disposing of his own wife in the same violent manner as Millhouser—but he will not, secure now in the knowledge that such miscreance is the lot of every human being, regardless of his pretensions to being a "moral" person. If anything, Higgins is now in the position of being that better able to withstand the temptation to his previous severity. O'Hara's style is as clear and as minutely finished with regard to every exterior detail of the lives of his personages as any of Vermeer's genre studies. In *Ourselves to Know*, O'Hara exploits this same command in an effort to present by way of conversational re-creation and the interior monologue, what previously would have remained only in the form of conventional prose description. "I have often wondered," Higgins remarks, "as I watched newsreels of structural workers on skyscrapers and mountain climbers on precipices, what the anonymous cameraman was thinking and doing." As in none of the preceding novels, ". . . the story behind the story is relevant. . . ."

Thus, O'Hara once more fortunately returns to the calmness of descriptive interest, that is able to allow him to produce the sense of futility combined with the recognition of Millhouser's own sense of static disinterestedness. As the persona for such an attitude pushed to the extreme that it is in Higgins' visits to the house in Lyons. Millhouser's boredom only serves as the summation for the similar attitudes of any of O'Hara's other protagonists. His life has reached its greatest peak of tragedy in the unfaithfulness of Hedda Steele. The anticlimatic series of sequels to this relationship constitutes the novel's most important statement of Robert Millhouser regarding the bitter lesson he has learned that love, because it is a relationship conducted between two average (and therefore fallible) human beings is bound to fail eventually for both partners. The best that love can provide, both as Millhouser and Higgins discover, is the merest physical outlet. To venture beyond this point is to invite destruction of the relationship. This may even be for the better—as it is the very act of prolongation which creates only the negative dividends of animosity, suspicion, dissatisfaction and boredom. Chester Calthorp, who later converts to Catholicism and joins a monastic order, is in no worse a position than Millhouser after his release from prison. Each of them ". . . in the cell of himself is almost convinced of his freedom" [39]—only the most surfaceous aspects of human life possess any ultimate sense of a source of infallible judgment. Millhouser's recollection on the days in prison predatory to his acquittal might be just as descriptive of his state of mind at any other phase of his life: ". . . I know up here, in my brain, that there are certain things I ought to do. Polite things. But instead of feelings I have this numbness. I've been waiting ever since I was brought here for the regrets or the remorse, the contrition, the penitence. It won't come. . . ." After this, the only differences between one form of imprisonment and the other—Millhouser's consignment to the perpetual sense of his failure at the hands of his mother and his wife—are the material comforts of Millhouser's station and the relationship he observes with Gerald Higgins. His redaction of his tragedy is an *acte gratuit* which Millhouser can only indulge himself because of two reasons. One is his moral conviction that Higgins should guide his own life by the same principles of respect for the human tendency toward inevitable moral decline. The other is his own need to state this belief to himself as apothegm. Only by so doing can Millhouser retain any resignation to this tragic generality. O'Hara's allusion to Pope's *Essay on Man* can thus be interpreted in its most cynical but also, stoically speaking, in its most rewarding sense.

III. The Stories

LIONEL TRILLING declares in an Introduction to a compilation of O'Hara's short stories that it is only on the basis of the author's "passionate commitment to verisimilitude . . ." [40] of social distinctions that O'Hara stands or falls as a generist in the short story medium. While it is only too easy to point to a great many of these stories as being expressive of the doctrine of a certain kind of social naturalism, it has until now remained a sadly neglected phase of scholarship and criticism that O'Hara's theme often consists of considerably more than such alone. This is to say that many of the better stories (especially those contained in the Trilling collection) express a vision of reality which at times makes the social temper of certain of these appear trivial by way of comparison. The best (and the longest) of these stories embody a vision of the futility of human effort in the face not only of the hostility of social demand, but, beyond this, the ineffably dark and unknowable forces of a universe itself even more violent in its capacity to defeat the luckiest of us. In such fine stories as *Summer's Day, The Doctor's Son, Over the River and Through the Wood, The Decision,* O'Hara begins with the realities—and impossibilities—of class mobility—but *finishes,* after exploiting to the utmost their maximal pungence of verisimilitude, by presenting us with his

46

tragic sense of the meanness of reality itself. It is also not of minor importance that O'Hara has cast his characters in these better stories as being from the uppermost ranges of the social compost heap. It is O'Hara's intention (not only as an inversion of his personal sadism) to demonstrate to his readers that even the Very Rich must suffer undue punishment at the hands of unmanageable destiny. O'Hara is always bringing to bear the overwhelming intensity of his focus upon the periphery of the wall of our isolation, which only takes the most elemental form as it reveals itself in mannerisms, affectations and habits. Among these are the judgments of one's intellect. True, O'Hara as a social commentator whose ". . . characteristic way of representing the elemental [in human nature] is through its modification by social circumstance . . ." [41] is the typical outlook on the part of most of the discerning critical intelligentsia. At least, such has been the tendency of Charles Poor, Lionel Trilling, Edmund Wilson and John Woodburn. Only a varied amount of positive criticism (and this dedicated to the novels alone) extrapolates from this basic groundwork toward any realization of a more cosmic ideal in O'Hara as a short-story writer.

In fact, it is during O'Hara's moments of indulgence of the superfices of social realism that his work degenerates into a series of vignettes of the life of the characters being described, puny in view of their insignificance of any "theme." This theme may often amount to little more than the conclusion that a man's wife is chronically unfaithful—as in *Saffercisco,* or that it will only be *Days* before two people will commit adultery in a suburban setting. Such stories have their start and finish in the tiny bit of reality which they set out to describe but never lead to more than a manner of word-picture as their subject material. It is during such exercises as *Pershing or Ten Eyck, Ten Eyck or Pershing, Back in New Haven,* or *Invite*—all written in the first person as, respectively, a speech to a certain Delphian society, a diary entry, or a letter—that O'Hara's journalistic inclination is diverted into the medium of reportage for its own sake rather than reportage used in an effort to exceed itself in the interest of grave and poignant human document. The best of O'Hara's stories are laden with such exempla.

However, they will usually contain, incidentally speaking, any number of them, all of which may be summated into a series of concretions which underlie the essential meaning of a story. They represent the social circumstance alone, rather than how this circumstance may be seen to combine with several others of its own kind in modifying any representation of the elemental. Consider again Trilling's pursuit of this train of reasoning, as it applies to the story *Summer's Day*. This is a story dealing with the reactions of an older man toward the suicide of his daughter.

> . . . The story proceeds on a series of small observations which include the protocol of an exclusive beach club and the question of who is sitting on whose bench; the social position of Catholics; the importance of election to a Yale senior society; the kind of epicene gossip that well-brought-up adolescents might take pleasure in. And the elemental fact which we confront when the story comes to its end is a good deal more than what we blandly call bereavement, it yields an emotion much more terrible than grief —the father's knowledge that he has reached the end of manhood and that the nothingness of life has overtaken him.[42]

As these items accumulate, the sum total of their occurrence— proliferatively—makes for the story's final conviction of the belief expressed by Mr. Attrell that ". . . there was really nothing to face, really nothing." [43] As DeFoe anchors the gradual trend of Moll Flanders toward middleclass respectability in the bedrock of monetary substance, so does O'Hara allow each moment of depiction of the class-standing of every personage to eventuate in the final predicament of such as Attrell. The greatest moments in all of O'Hara's literary output occur as a result of his fusion of the graphic details in these short stories into the symbols which they collectively embody of a manner of despair common to every man. What therefore matters in the treatment of each story followed below is, primarily, the specific nature of the tragic emotion pointed out; and secondarily, O'Hara's use of the concrete and graphic indices of descriptive technique in rendering apparent this tragic realization.

Over the River and Through the Wood proceeds along

a surface of indices toward the final realization that a man named Mr. Winfield has grown old, and do what he may, grown ugly for no reason of his own. As in these other stories, the issue of aloneness finally pervades. The nursery-song title ironically applies to a sleigh-ride through Connecticut, at the end of which Mr. Winfield does little more than surprise one of the young ladies at her bath in the family manse.

It is only because Mr. Winfield performs an accident that he is defeated. This defeat consists of aggravating the already-present awareness of his personal unwantedness. Mr. Winfield and the reader cannot help but notice that his inclusion in the sleighing party is due only to an act of etiquette. It is never shown that anyone—neither Sheila, his granddaughter, nor her friends, nor even Ula, the maid—positively desires his presence for reasons of companionship or even amusement. "So it was sit outside and freeze or sit on the little seat inside." Not even when Mr. Winfield leaves a window open in the sleigh, while seated on the strapontin and creating an uncomfortable draft, do the girls immediately notice this physical discomfort. Sheila "closed the windows, not even acknowledging Mr. Winfield's shamed apologies." Upon arriving at the home, there is an omen cleverly revealed of what is to follow as "he went out to the darkened hall and Ula, the maid, jumped in fright. 'Ugh. Oh. It's you, Mr. Winfield. You like to scare me.' "

The only sense of happiness contrived by Mr. Winfield is during his isolation within his bedroom. Here, at least, he is free to reflect, as he sits like Joe Chapin in his den, "humming old songs, sipping watered whiskey and reviewing his life." Mr. Winfield is alone, and for the time being at least, is able to see his way of life as offering little better than this recollective sense of mentally re-ordering the memories of his situation. This, and the sense of physical well-being which he enjoys partaking of: "Little touches, ashtrays, flowers . . . ," the chocolate he drinks, which "made him a little thirsty, but it was good and warming, and Mary was right; it was better than a drink." But even this cannot last. O'Hara now takes us into a reportial exegesis of the condition of Mr. Winfield's family home. His daughter's husband has bought the house, and Mr. Winfield, no longer wealthy, has had to give in. The dimension of O'Hara's social-class depiction is enacted in the humiliation Mr. Winfield must acknowledge, as it is specified in monetary terms, as frigidly impersonal as in the very legal contract itself. His son-in-law has told him, "I'll pay the delinquent taxes myself and give you a hundred and fifty thousand dollars for the house and grounds." In other words, Mr. Winfield ". . . was 'protecting' them all over again, by selling his house so that he would not become a family charge—protecting the very same people from the embarrassment of a poor relation." Mr. Winfield has been deserted by all those who might have been close to him at one time, and even before his catastrophic *faux pas,* would be only too happy to live out the rest of his years in this at least physically comfortable interior, remote from the intervention of unfeeling humanity and nature itself.

It is purely by circumstance that Mr. Winfield's mishap takes shape. Ula, the maid, has left two cups upon a tray for Mr. Winfield's chocolate. During the ride, Mr. Winfield has listened with some intensity to the conversation of his daughter and her friends. One of them is Kay Farnsworth. Mr. Winfield suddenly realizes that she is the most interesting person he has met in many dull years. On the basis of the overheard conversation, he decides that "It would be fun to talk to her, to sound her out and see how far she had progressed toward, say, ambition or disillusionment." If for this once only, he feels that he must invite her to have cocoa with him, "As former master of this house."

By accident the maid has left an extra cup on the tray. And it is by accident, more likely than not the result of deafness brought on by his own senility, that Mr. Winfield mistakes the girl's "In a minute" for "come in." He opens the door to discover her practically naked. "There was cold murder in the girl's eyes, and loathing and contempt and the promise of the thought his name forever would evoke. She spoke to him: 'Get out of here, you dirty old man.' " Insult is added to the already standing injury long inimical to Mr. Winfield's pride. *Over the River and Through the Wood,* besides being as descriptive as it is of Mr. Winfield's introspective solitude, is thus a statement

of how an ordinary—and by the less socially exalted of us, forgivably trivial—mistake can be to one's undoing. As at Joe
Chapin's funeral, ". . . Friends [could] bore you as much as
enemies, and the ones quickly became the other over nothing
more important than a near-sighted revoke at bridge. . . ." Mr.
Winfield has been driven back into the confinement which he
has had no desire to partake of, by behaving naively. All during
the story, every person has behaved supremely in accordance
with the code of his class—either as master or servant. It is a
petty and self-righteous caste of society which Kay Farnsworth
represents, in view of her total lack of deference in the presence
of an older gentleman. Mr. Winfield can now do little better
than face the realization that "there was all the time in the
world, too much of it, for him. He knew it would be hours before he would begin to hate himself. For a while he would just
sit there and plan his own terror."

Decision is a story prelusive of the thesis stated by Higgins in Ourselves to Know, that isolation from society is the
ultimate fate of any of us who will stand face to face with our
own essence—social forces can affect us up to a point (particularly in view of O'Hara's emphasis upon the aspects of vertical
mobility)—but once we become inured to their operation beyond ourselves, we are forced into the contemplation of why
we behave as we do—in regard to these elements. This is why
O'Hara can say with utmost certitude that "my characters have
two patterns. One is superficial . . . the other is psychological."
In Decision, the social forces of family censure force Francis
Townsend into the remoteness of his home, never to travel outside of Gibbsville, never to marry, and never to practice medicine. His uncle, upon Townsend's graduation from medical
school, informs him that because his parents both died in mental institutions, he may neither practice nor marry. His uncle
says to him, " 'You won't have to worry about money. I've fixed
that at the bank. Give yourself plenty of time to pick and
choose. You'll decide on something.' . . . 'Oh, very likely I will,'
Francis said. 'I won't just stay on here in the village.' But that,
it turned out, was what he did decide to do." Francis Townsend is rendered the victim of a now outmoded system of psy-

chology. While it may be generally regarded today that insanity need not be considered transmissible by heredity, the uncle of Francis Townsend stands for those forces of social reaction, one step away from superstition in their dogma. Although from a distinguished background, Townsend cannot accept his position in such a milieu without being forced into the concomitant resignation to the demands of outer authority that he submit or suffer an even worse fate than to be an M.D. without a practice.

Decision gives one a sense of material gratification—in regard to the sensate objects depicted by O'Hara—especially the interior furnishings of Francis Townsend's abode—which is made that much more instrumental to the purpose of the story by the feeling they create of their unvarying mundaneness. Every material detail is rendered as poignant—that is, as unpoignant—as Townsend's own fate. The lifelessness of these objects presents a humble and somber backdrop to the everyday rounds of Francis Townsend as he spends his day from getting out of bed at 6:30, to taking his walk, to going to his place at the village bar, until he returns home that night, to read from the 19th-century novels in his library—"till it was time to bank the kitchen fire for the next morning and finish off the last of the wrapped bottle of rye." The sturdy and well-finished physical objects stand by impersonally while Townsend lives on. "The home of Francis Townsend could have been taken for the birthplace of a nineteenth-century American poet, one of those little white houses by the side of the road that are regarded by the interested as national shrines. . . ." It is the feeling of unvarying habit, created by O'Hara's command of interior genre, which provides insight into the blankness of Townsend's existence. As in a Dutch interior, all the objects in the central still-life composition which stand in the middle of the home being described, stand out in their objective arrangement—artificial but nevertheless there—while through the window or doorway can be seen the vacant and airy nothingness of exterior reality. Such is Townsend's given condition—to live amid these physical realities and see in their enduring solidarity the contrast to so ephemeral a manner of suffering as his own. Townsend will at any rate accept his defeat bravely, and with grace.

The Chink in the Armor is a study in snobbery and the life of those who perpetually practice this vice. However, even Chauncy Wayne is not safe. This is because even though he may appear safe from censure from any person beneath his exalted social station, it is within his own stratum that he must expect and be on guard against the nemesis of social disapproval. No one is safe from snobbery—not even those at the very apex of the social-class pyramid. Mr. Wayne lives on an income in a private apartment in New York which is furnished with ancestral portraits and even with family armor. Nevertheless, the armor may impress many but not those members of Mr. Wayne's coterie who know one of his innermost personal secrets. Metaphorically, this is the chink in the armor—a silver cigarette box, the existence of which renders the armor a thing of solely antiquarian value, incapable any longer of being of practical use to Mr. Wayne in New York in the 1950's. To those of tantamount arrangement in the social hierarchy as Mr. Wayne (not to mention those even higher), Wayne is merely one-of-a-kind —no better, no worse.

The story involves Chauncy Wayne's hour of moral triumph. For once, anyway, he feels that he has "the edge" over a contemporary. This is a young man, the son of another who knows that Wayne has bought and presented himself with a silver cigarette box, inscribed with the names of the members of a billiard team. The father of Ted Crow is anathema to Wayne because of his knowledge of the latter's indulgence of his own vanity. In *The Chink in the Armor* (as in many others), the issue of personal vengeance looms large in the motivation of Chauncy Wayne. He invites Crow to his apartment to warn him against dropping out of an exclusive Manhattan Club. It is because, however, of Wayne's exaltedness of breeding and complete confidence in the unalterable status of his position, that he can advise Crow for his own good. To hold a grudge against Ted Crow because of his father's knowledge would be the epitome of debasement to the same moral (and speaking in terms of minute gradations), social, level of conduct. Wayne's

effort at magnanimity in advising the younger man is one of
O'Hara's most significant ventures into the depiction of social
snobbery. Not only is *The Chink in the Armor* documentary
of the variety of life among the Very Rich to be lived while
poised on razor's edge while in fear of discovery of the family
"skeleton in the closet." It is also demonstrative of a kind of
snobbery particular to a given, if rarefied, section of the *haute
monde*. Such is not the case in another *Hellbox* story, *Other
Women's Households*. Here, a young married couple bitterly
acknowledge their submission to the principal stockholder of
the town bank who refuses to see the wife on the grounds of her
flaunting of the mores of the local bourgeoisie. Such is no less
the case with Julian English, still so uncertain of his place in
society that he must condescend to throw a drink in the face of
an upstart. *The Chink in the Armor* presents a more subtle
embodification of the snobbery not of a man who is on the
move but one who is already there. Mr. Wayne's form of con-
descension is the product of unnumbered generations. Mr.
Wayne can consider impersonally the issue of social dero-
gation as a thing of will. He knows by his middle age (regardless of his former days at Princeton, when Crow's father "was
the dirt under his feet, especially during Bicker Week") that to
snub another human is to his own moral discredit, and not to
that of the snubbed. O'Hara presents the social difference between the two generations as being simply this—one takes the
issue of personal vengeance seriously enough to advise his son
somehow to remind Wayne of his previous malfeasance—the
other remains far above such rancor. It is, to Mr. Wayne, mer-
etricious of the best possibilities in a man. Even so, he will
devour his Christmas pudding and enjoy it as well. Mr. Wayne
lectures Ted Crow tactfully on the topic of his adulterous relations with the wife of a fellow club member. It becomes subtly
apparent that Mr. Wayne is enough Crow's superior as regards
age as well as social standing to do so with authority and impunity. As the story comes to a finish, Mr. Wayne shows Crow
around the apartment. The two approach Mr. Wayne's dressing
room, in which is located the ominous silver cigarette box.
". . . Mr. Wayne did not lead the way into the room. 'That

about does it,' he said. He was obviously trying to guess whether
Ted had seen the silver box, and if so, whether the box meant
anything to him. He held out his hand and adroitly led Ted to
the hall door. . . ." Mr. Wayne has had his moment of revenge
through his own magnanimous and efficacious handling of the
situation.

This same recurrent motif of the resolution of the desire
for personal revenge appears thematically in many of the short
stories. Notable examples are *The Chink in the Armor, Someone to Trust, All the Girls He Wanted,* and *Price's Always
Open.* In each of these stories, O'Hara makes the very most of
the score that must be settled. Regardless of life's essential
meaninglessness, the protagonist must be able to retain the
sense of his own potency over and against those who would
deny him such in the interests of his indignity. Doubtless, psy-
chologically speaking, O'Hara's millionaires satisfy the same
need for the author to attain this sense of power, if without the
activation to stoop to a fisticuffs or telling another person to
his face that his is a gratuitous existence. Life, because it is
difficult for any personage created by O'Hara, has only these
two ephemeral sources of reward: the gratification of tactile or
gustatory stimulus by physical wellbeing (as in *Decision*), or
the sense of temporary moral victory over an adversary, of getting the edge. *Someone to Trust,* for example, is a story dealing
with an out-of-work entertainer on the hideout from a criminal
mob. His former mistress is by now about to marry another
man as soon as Tommy Welting arrives in New York. He manages to take refuge in her apartment and then burns a photo-
graph of the girl's new lover. Against the imperturbable forces
of his own misfortune, Welting is somehow able to enjoy the
intense if fleeting joy of his satisfaction of revenge. In keeping
with O'Hara's contention that since life's rewards are all of
little endurance, one can at least enjoy the temporary moral
satisfaction of getting the edge on one's tormentors. It is purely
a question of time before the evil ones finally and completely
win out. In a matter of months, Tommy Welting may be dead
at the hands of hired murderers. He can meanwhile recoup the

belief in his own pride. " 'A man could stay here forever, if he had to,' he told himself."

All the Girls He Wanted, in like manner, is a study in a woman's recollections of a young man with whom she at one time commenced to have an affair, then after reneging, learns that her best friend has taken up where she herself left off. Her moment of triumph occurs after learning that the young man, Cliff Kizer, has been brutally mangled to death in an auto wreck. The woman begins by reflecting upon the grotesque nature of his death. ". . . They had taken life out of him and left him in a car that did not catch fire. They—God—had not even burned him up with fire, but had left his terrible broken body for anyone to see. Frances hugged herself. . . ." *All the Girls He Wanted* also uses a device of allowing Frances' speculations on Kizer—before and after his death—to succeed each other as they occur in the mind of this woman, irrespective of objective chronological sequence. This is why, at the end of the story, Frances' learning that her friend has been deceived into having her affair by Kizer, now dead after the most painful manner of infliction, only can make her extremely happy to have been able to picture him lying dead. The bestial in Frances, as in all of us, makes for the story's climax on a note of optimism. She, too, has gained the upper hand for a moment. The story ends as Frances is able to say to herself that she is a "lucky, lucky girl."

Edmund Wilson refers to *Price's Always Open* as the one story in which "the forces of democracy finally win out." [44] Which is to say that it is a story of social class conflict. It nevertheless has in common with many of the other stories this vengeance motif, if placed in a social setting. By means of threatening the summer crowd (after he has knocked a man unconscious), Price is able to get the better of a social superior. This same young man has kicked a man knocked down in a fight, and sees fit to do the same to Price's summer counterman, a student at Holy Cross. The story very effectively achieves its sense of justice along with whatever elements of vengeance O'Hara wishes to characterize in Mr. Price. One wonders, however, in doing justice to Wilson's statement, whether, as is usual to O'Hara, Price emerges victorious, in view of the story's ending as follows: ". . . thinking it over, Mr. Price agreed with himself that those would be the last sounds he ever expected to hear from the summer crowd."

The Doctor's Son is the first in a series of several stories (and two novels, Butterfield 8 and Hope of Heaven) which employ as their protagonist James Malloy, son of a Gibbsville doctor. Throughout the development of O'Hara's fictional style, Jim Malloy, like no other major character, serves as the personification of the author himself. Other O'Hara heroes—Julian English, Sidney Tate, Joe Chapin, and so on—represent less an embodiment of Hara's own person—autobiographically presented—than they do the result of O'Hara's observation of them from without, controlled and modified by the intensity of O'Hara's moral judgment. O'Hara has chosen these characters for the depiction of them much as F. Scott Fitzgerald might be described in the words of Malcolm Cowley, "as if at the same time he stood outside the ballroom, the little midwestern boy with his nose to the glass, wondering how much the tickets cost and who paid for the music." He writes of such people in the knowledge that his social and aesthetic distance from them enables rather than hinders a sense of objectivity as the result of remoteness. Malloy, on the other hand, is shown to be from Northeastern Pennsylvania, the son of well-to-do (if not munificent) parents. As the stories continually reappear, he is shown as not going to college (O'Hara's regret at not attending Yale is by now the salient feature of most biographers' squibs which refer to his life before the publication of Appointment in Samarra), working as a reporter, and finally as a script-writer in Hollywood. There could be no more directly autobiographic redaction of O'Hara's own exposure to the horror of death by disease in Gibbsville during an epidemic of influenza to those in the mining section and to the father of Malloy's girl. This is followed by Malloy's learning of the scandal of adultery between her mother and the substitute doctor. Malloy is able to avoid the injury of class-snobbery throughout his life.

... What I want to say, what I started out to explain was why I said, "you people, you members of the upper crust," and so on, implying that I am not a member of it. Well, I'm *not* a member of it. ...

His only canon for social standing lies in the middle-class standard of ability which particularly—as in *Hope of Heaven*—is reflected by means of monetary earning power. This is why Malloy writes for the films. More important, however, this emphasis upon cold cash as the sole agent of purchase of the symbols of wealth—the deliberate insistence upon Malloy's immediately acknowledging to himself that recently acquired wealth, not inherited, makes for a social difference—is the essential undercurrent in *Transaction*, a story in the *Hellbox* series. Malloy recognizes that social classes will and must exist in society. He is the spokesman for O'Hara's stoically conservative—and what any number of critics will doubtless refer to as snobbishly reactionary—stand in favor of class distinction as being revelatory of the best in humankind, even while O'Hara's other protagonists, as they appear in his novels, can be seen to embody and bring out the worst. Malloy can choose his friends and mistresses as he sees fit, on the basis of their personal attractiveness, exclusive of their parents' or their own Dun and Bradstreet rating. Such is the case with the women presented in *Butterfield 8* and *Hope of Heaven*. Malloy remains on the periphery of society at all elevations—much like Pal Joey, that "night-creature" so described by Lionel Trilling—always observing, never forgetful, but impervious to what can affect others less worldly (and less flush) than himself.

The Doctor's Son reminds one almost immediately of Hemingway's Nick Adams stories, particularly *Indian Camp*. In both, a boy accompanies an older person to a treatment of patients in squalid surroundings. Jim Malloy and Nick Adams thus undergo their first eyewitness contact with death by unnatural causes. There is also an interesting parallel between Malloy's recollection that after losing his girl, he "never can remember her married name" and Adams' suddenly remembering, also at the end of the story, that "his heart was not broken" in *Ten Indians*.[46] Both boys have experienced much by their early teens, but have emerged whole in spite of it. For O'Hara, however, *The Doctor's Son* involves the transplantation of Nick Adams' Michigan countryside into Gibbsville. Its chief appeal as a story lies in its Gibbsvillian topography which O'Hara makes one with the main item of Jim Malloy's maturity, so suddenly enforced upon him. Malloy has discovered that death can occur in a distasteful fashion—and even to those one is intimately concerned for. Not only this, but that same Mr. Evans has been the object of his wife's unfaithfulness. The impact of these events so overwhelms and innures Malloy, that the issue of his girl's departure recedes only too obviously before these shocks. Malloy has suddenly become an adult. He is "only surprised [but not overwhelmed]" when Edith Evans elopes.

The Doctor's Son is actually a story more given to tactile and graphic attention to its setting than many of the later stories. There is nevertheless in the story *Transaction* an insight into the mature Malloy, now become a successful script writer after *Hope of Heaven,* who is in Cambridge to pay for a Duesenberg limousine. His meeting with the married couple makes for a study in depiction of the minutiae of class difference and the stand Malloy takes in regard to it.

Much of *Transaction* consists of description for its own intrinsic interest of the details of the interior of the home lived in by the couple, as well as their habits, mannerisms, artifacts. These are the Van Burens. The wife

> . . . straightened her back, after the manner, possibly, of a dowager aunt. This girl, Malloy knew, was a lady. She was nearly a generation away from certain friends of his, but he was sure that if he started the do-you-know game there would be a tumbling forth of names—aunts and uncles, cousins and parents of her friends. . . .

As Charles Van Buren, the husband, comes in to find Malloy and his wife talking together, he says to both of them

> . . . trying to be jovial [that they are] "drinking their heads off, bag packed, I suppose I'll find a note on the pillow." . . . "Yes and look at the bag. Louis Vuitton," she said. . . . "Naturally it'd be a man with money," said Van Buren. There was no bitterness in

the way he said it, but it was not the thing to say, and they all knew it. . . .

Then, as Malloy presents Van Buren with the check, Malloy notices that the car now has a spotlight which he insists upon paying for. This is the most important point in the story (occurring as it does in most of O'Hara's), near the end. He writes out another check for seventy-five dollars, and the transaction is concluded. Malloy sees the Duesenberg as a symbol of the life he wishes to become accustomed to. More than this, however, he would rather pay cold cash for the extra fixture because he is not ashamed to admit to the Van Burens that his intimacy with the mechanical and economic fixtures of a Duesenberg is something which he owns up to and will not avoid merely for the sake of social courtesy. Malloy sees an expensive Duesenberg as a symbol, but also as a reality. He is never afraid to point out to others, as O'Hara himself does, if less explicitly in his fiction, that it is not enough only to dress and talk in a cherished manner. To do so by itself is a form of grossest hypocrisy. Money must remain the responsible agent, even for Van Buren, whose "buttoned-down collar of his shirt was a little frayed, as though he had done an incomplete job with nail scissors." It will likewise remain so for Malloy himself, who may one day marry and rear a son who is elected to a Yale senior society.

Miss W. follows *Transaction* in the *Hellbox* collection. The story concerns Miss Woodberry, who teaches at a girls' junior college and at the time of the story is signing in girls back from weekend vacation. One of them is late and has not reported back. She finally is returned by Malloy in the same Duesenberg. The girl has been in a slight accident. Miss Woodberry is surprised to meet Malloy, who is an old friend. Again, one gets the feeling that Malloy's entire life consists of driving about the countryside near exclusive schools and colleges in his Duesenberg, secure in the knowledge that his earning power has enabled him to do so. His performance of the slight favor is part of the magnanimity due to such a station. It is "For old times' sake," as he explains to Miss Woodberry, who gives Malloy a free meal. The final moment of triumph is Malloy's. He

is only too happy to recollect and review his former days, as he
sits in Miss Woodberry's study. She notes,

> . . . "Here we sit, fat and middle-aged, me chewing on one side
> of my mouth because I'm afraid of losing a filling. . . . It's not
> too bad." Malloy says nothing. "Well, at least we can pretend it
> isn't." "Right," he said.

Malloy wants only to enjoy his series of remembrances, although
there is a hint in his final reply, of still dormant sexual attraction.

Following *Transaction* is the last story in *Hellbox, Conversation in the Atomic Age*. Seen superficially, it is a deft and
satiric record of nothing more than a lunchtime conversation
between Malloy and a Los Angeles society woman, set in Hollywood. Its location in *Hellbox* may be seen as a coda to the depiction of O'Hara—Malloy. While the woman, Mrs. Schmidt,
does most of the talking, it is Malloy, who, secure in view of his
social position because he has "paid his way" as a successful
screen-writer, can talk to her exactly as he pleases. However,
he realizes that to remind her of her inanity would only be to
touch on too sensitive a spot. Malloy is only too interested in
watching Mrs. Schmidt give herself away; by the end of the
story it even is conceivable that Malloy is using her as material
for another film. He may be slightly flip, but never rude or even
in earnest. This would be to curtail Malloy's own contemplation. Finally, Malloy looks across at another table to notice the
wife of a good friend at lunch with another man. Malloy can
only respond by taking home his luncheon guest. He has seen
all that he might want to see that afternoon, or any other afternoon. He is shown as avoiding any form of positive participation
which might affect the purity of his vision, even in the interests
of a good friend. He may write it out of his system, but he will
not consider willful action.

As a stylist in the short story medium, John O'Hara at
times comes close to a more poignant and literal command of
his material than in even the best of his novels. O'Hara's most
outstanding defect—artistically speaking, his most flagrant sin
of commission—is his tendency never to know when to stop,

particularly in his tactile and visual descriptions of social class insignia. There are times *A Rage to Live* offers the most compelling instance of this—at which the subtle and intricate psychological motivation of a character becomes overshadowed by O'Hara's equally attentive redaction of what he or she has eaten for breakfast or the details of one's living-room interior. In the short stories, however, the reader is never aware of such excesses. Every one of the descriptions of such similar items *(vide A Summer's Day)* adds somewhat, if only minutely, to the gradual accumulation of the realm of the major theme. "Just what is the purpose of these extraneous diversions?" asks Edmund Wilson, writing seven years after the appearance of *Appointment in Samarra*. Not so, as regards the finer short stories of O'Hara. These more capably allow O'Hara himself more efficaciously to sublimate his at times insatiable urge in the direction of description for its own sake into meaningful symbolism, valuable as much for its quaintness of sociological insight as for the light it sheds on a story's final statement of any character's predicament. Thus, such particulars gradually snowball into a total impression created by the realization of a major chord. That "the description is never gratuitous or for its own sake" [48] can hardly be denied the stories, even though one often demands this same of the longer ventures into prose fiction.

If there are any salient and always predictable qualities to the fiction of John O'Hara, one of these would have to consist of his pessimistic awareness of the helpless despair of the sensitive individual in the face of a hierarchic social system. Trilling compares O'Hara to Kafka, insofar as both writers recognize that it is always easy to make the one fatal mistake in one's everyday life which will set into motion against himself the mechanism of the social machinery which impersonally is responsible for that individual's survival but could, in such cases, be as equally effective in sealing his doom. This, plus the theory, somewhat existentialist in its own way, of the "Hellbox" or private suffering of each of us, regardless of his social attitudes, resulting from the conflict between individual nature, or idiosyncrasy, and the inhibitions enacted by the hostility of reality itself. Every man has to suffer, O'Hara is continually implying; yet this must be in his own way and by himself. No other party can share in the privateness of this hell. Every man is an island.

The stories, at their best, convey O'Hara's conviction of pessimism in a direct and, unlike the novels, condensed, manner of statement. At their worst, they appear purely anecdotal beside O'Hara's more serious examples, only as vignettes or individual monologues. But O'Hara is never so much in command of the situation as when he can, like a Flemish miniaturist, present a household interior in all its graphically precise realism, in the midst of which a man or woman sits alone with his or her memories and sensations, ultimately impervious either to these tactile realities or even to whatever other persons may be sharing this reality being set down. A good example would be the story *The Cold House*. While it may lack the conviction of *The Decision* or any of the stories described above, this story's greatest merit inheres in its capacity to suggest visually to its reader that this home is Mrs. Carnavon's private inferno, as real as any of the objects with which she feels herself immured. Near the very end, "She saw herself . . . how to love." *The Cold House* exemplifies well O'Hara's concern with the description of the "crypt of useless things"—and the knowledge that these useless things will never assuage the death of a son.

IV. Summary

It would not constitute an injustice to either writer to compare John O'Hara with F. Scott Fitzgerald. Not only does O'Hara own up to the influence (not to mention that of Tarkington, Hemingway, Rolland, Galsworthy, and Howells), but there are, as a result, various obvious effects of this. Both authors deal with the frustrations of the desire for increased class mobility on the parts of such alike characters as Joe Chapin and Jay Gatsby. There exists in these two an emphasis upon Original Sin as the source of the final moral degradation of such as Alfred Eaton, and both Richard Diver and Anthony Patch. A third area of appreciable resemblance inheres in the fact that, as a result of this hypostatization of the Original Sin concept, almost every protagonist in the novels and stories of both Fitzgerald and O'Hara is shown as being forced to undergo defeat at the hands of an impossibly severe social code of moral severity. The characters are actually no better than the impersonal forces of sexual attraction and the vanity of their need for social advancement. In neither Fitzgerald nor O'Hara does there occur the capacity for any individual, heroically speaking, to get the better of himself and his mean ambition. The setting in the midst of the *haute bourgeoisie* is the source of the material about which both of these writers will choose an attitude of

64

precise prose depiction to be further tempered by the moralistic indignation of the "Spoiled Priest."

It is more in the perception of differences between these two than in their similarity that the aims of O'Hara as a moral commentator upon the ways of the Smart Set become more visible.

The greatest difference between them is that O'Hara is given over to displaying the interior psychology of the rich, and thereby the emotional sufferings of even the wealthiest and most eminent of these. The socially prominent and their inferiors alike have their troubles—and find life tragic. F. Scott Fitzgerald, on the other hand, prefers to display the Very Rich —as in *The Great Gatsby*—as being perpetually in a state of impugnable and riotous self-indulgence. The rich of F. Scott Fitzgerald can at least retain some sensation (*vide The Diamond As Big As the Ritz*) of both their feckless domination over all other social classes that are beneath them, and the glories of physical titillation. To be rich is to be happy, to F. Scott Fitzgerald. To be rich is to be no better off than to be poor or middle-class, to O'Hara.

Even though both condemn the excesses of the classes they depict, F. Scott Fitzgerald never manages to fathom the suffering of the rich people who oppose the protagonists of his novels. Even though Nicole Diver appears as a case of distorted sexuality from early in childhood (as does Gloria Wandrous in *Butterfield 8*), she can still indulge her desire for anything she wants by marrying her psychiatrist, and with equal dispatch, upon regaining her mental health, divorce him. In the novels of O'Hara, all the people regardless of social class who appear in any appreciable role at all, are shown to be fighting some interior battle with themselves and are usually, by the same token, only capable at disparate moments, of satisfying their sensual instincts. These characters are always in the process of holding some interior monologue with themselves, in an effort, however futile, to come to grips with some earlier emotional problem or to disregard temporarily the reality of seemingly inadequate social station.

The sentiment of antisnobbery is a paramount issue to

both Fitzgerald and O'Hara. In the work of one, the reader is made to feel sympathy for even the most treacherous of those who are set against such heroes as Julian English or Robert Millhouser. O'Hara, especially by means of displaying a "villainous" character's past life, attempts the objective portrayal of the forces causing his snobbery, and strives for an attitude of being able to forgive through being able to understand. In Fitzgerald, there exists a more two-dimensional emphasis upon the social snob in high societal position as being villainous by inclination, and not by the force of formative events.

Although all this is not to say that F. Scott Fitzgerald is the lesser artist, it is only to point out that his genius is a matter of being able to depict the situation created by his characters, if at the same time paying less attention to the intensity of these characters' inner struggle with issues that are not always so relevant to the denouement of tragic realization as in his novels or such stories as *May Day, The Rich Boy,* or *Babylon Revisited.*

Not only, to quote again from Delmore Schwartz, does O'Hara's ". . . snob-sensitivity provide him with inexhaustible energy for the transformation of observation into fiction. . . ." O'Hara is a snob, but only this as a superficial revelation of his sadism which he transforms into the vision he presents of life on the uppermost levels of the American upper-crust. "It was neither accident nor invention which made him call the scapegoat of his first novel, Julian English; for English is an Anglo-Saxon, he resents the Irish. . . ." It was also no accident that Julian English, like Brock Caldwell or Joe Chapin, dies a premature and tragic death. In exactly the same vein, both of O'Hara's later novelistic protagonists—Alfred Eaton and Robert Millhouser—do not die, but are respectively victimized either by ignominious personal disgrace or the naked, blinding certitude of life's arrant meaninglessness.

The final means of comparison with F. Scott Fitzgerald resides in the fact that while Fitzgerald's attitude toward his heroes, at least, is compassion, O'Hara's is suppressed contempt. O'Hara indulges every opportunity to display his people in positions of indignity, death, and defeat. The prevailing emotion behind the emotion of snobbery itself is one of antagonism toward the universe and all its human inhabitants. O'Hara's particular position in the dialectic between cosmic optimism (as in, say, Tolstoi's conception of outer determinism as an act of the revelation of the mind of a benevolent deity) and unchallengeable gloom as man's lot on this piece of burned-off cinder —derives from the personal attitude of his manner of aggression. Snob that O'Hara may be, it is as a sadist first and as a snob afterward that he creates a situation where someone is snubbed. The vision O'Hara creates of the inner workings of the American "Power Elite," as in *From the Terrace* and elsewhere, may be as close to reality as that of any apologist for the inevitability of economic individualism since Theodore Dreiser or Frank Norris. However, much as O'Hara may overtly detest the manner in which such a system will crush all those who either stand in its way or can never measure up to its standards, he is only too content impassively to force Alfred Eaton to go under as much by virtue of a hypersensitive conscience as by exposure to the iniquities of highest-level conservative politics. Indeed, the prime fault of this very novel is a matter of O'Hara's rampant sadism which knows so few bounds that it allows the material to run away from the more essential theme of Eaton's guilt fixation.

O'Hara's basic attitude of hostility, resentment toward all those who are socially "well off," never lets up all through the succession of his novels, though his punishment meted out to his protagonists takes the form of less violent—though equally tragic—convictions of their own worthlessness. The substance of O'Hara's fiction, particularly as regards his plot objectification of the events which occur there, is always an act of sublimated sadism. This is not to gainsay the statement made above that O'Hara's manner of plumbing the emotional depths of as many characters as possible in any given work of fiction is an attempt to convey to the reader an attitude of sympathy toward such. It is to O'Hara's credit that he can so well create from the bias of his own sadism a multitude of characters, each one seen into so clearly in terms of the author's tragic certitude.

John O'Hara is not the most unctuous (nor the most amiable) of correspondents on his own work. Needless to say, his by now legendary mannerisms of personal hostility toward even the most friendly and tactful of his inquisitors must be interpreted as representing an extension of the attitude of suppressed contempt toward the specimens of humanity represented in his fiction. Nevertheless, O'Hara, by means of, and not in spite of, his aggression, allows each person to interact upon the other on the assumption that each, like himself, has a score to settle which only he as an individual can know and come to grips with. As a prose naturalist always striving to suggest like Balzac in the *Comedie Humaine* the moral issue of class-consciousness—the lesson that snobbery can and does result in evil for all concerned—it is necessary first of all for O'Hara to create the situation that must needs be interpreted so negatively by his readers. O'Hara must begin by showing an act of snobbery in all its viciousness, as he does, for example, in *Appointment in Samarra*. He finishes, however, by proving as he does, that after his dissection of the motives of such as Julian English snobbery, too, is a thing of futility because it is a thing of will. In this way one can acknowledge with compassion the reason for a character's (and O'Hara's) disgust with his lot and thereby his hostility to others.

The early doctrine regarding Original Sin thus pertains here. A man only possesses the power for good because he also possesses that for evil; he cannot be perfect enough to do only good works that are independent of the same capability for evil.

The "Hellbox" mechanism in O'Hara consists of the delineation of an individual's confinement to the pain of his recollections of his past life—and some event or events which have led to the effect of such upon his temperament and character. It is up to such a person either to survive by persevering as courageously as possible, in the midst of it, or as is more usually the case, go under in defeat by way of either death or humiliation. In the novels, the latter is unvaryingly the case, except as in the case of Robert Millhouser, protagonist of *Ourselves to Know*. Millhouser at least refuses to allow the severity of his feelings to result in diversionist behavior which will result in the depletion of his dignity as an individual human being. He takes for granted the tenuity of all hope of happiness on earth.

Unlike Dr. Townsend in *The Decision*, Millhouser wants only to contemplate his painfully acquired sense of certitude in this one thesis of despair. He does not drink as does Dr. Townsend, whose entire function is to forget, and not face his despair in the manner of Millhouser.

The thematic importance of such a character as Townsend is to point up the pessimism of most of O'Hara's people who cannot accept the futility of their own vision. Most of these temporarily hope to refute any such conviction, as they resort to some means of such necessary deception in the form of physical titillation—via sex or alcohol—or the establishment of a sense of false emotional security through their prehensile manner of maintaining a sense of exalted social mobility. As so many of O'Hara's characters proceed, like Julian English or Alfred Eaton, from one debauch to another, one gets the sense of their pathetic and by no means enviable need for as many distractions as possible. Only such superficial and temporary evidences of escape from the knowledge of life's despair make up the objective nature of most of the fiction.

Although the question of direct literary influence may be purely academic, there is, in the indebtedness O'Hara admits to Hemingway, more than the obvious one of emphasis upon the peripheral aspects of physical euphoria. "If it feels good afterwards, it feels good" can be seen as mutual sentiment in both writers. However, this apothegm only reflects the more inclusive one expressed by one of the waiters in *A Clean, Well-Lighted Place*, which is to the effect that a man who has plenty of money can be in despair about nothing. The cosmic boredom of the characters in both Hemingway and O'Hara is made to find its outlet as readily in Brett Ashley's profligacy as in that of Grace Tate. Julian English, as he throws his drink into the face of Harry Reilly, is motivated by the need to assert his allegiance with the social class to which he must toe the line. It is his only ambition. Likewise, Robert Cohn must compulsively put himself through his affair with Lady Brett to prove to himself that he can so successfully obtain the favors of an honest-to-goodness British countess. (So does Roger Bannon likewise pursue Grace Tate, as far as concerns his own need to over-whelm a female representative of a social class beyond his own.)

The revelations of such thematic kinship between the two authors—especially regarding the one of the need for relief from such excessive *ennui*—knows no bounds. Toward the present phase of O'Hara's fictional career, one cannot help but become aware of a new motivation for his emphasis upon the depiction of the life of the rich. It is this: that the greatest horror the reader becomes aware of in O'Hara's millionaires is that even for such materially privileged people life is no better than for anyone else. The rich are inhibited far more than their underlings, even though theirs may be a difference of emotional frustration in kind, rather than in degree.

Much as O'Hara may write from the psychological need to identify with members of such an economic and social milieu, his works, in time, begin to assert that he has surpassed the aspirations of such writers as J. P. Marquand or Tarkington, or any American or British "society" novelists. These are content only to represent the surface aspects of what it is to be a member of the *haute monde*. O'Hara wants to reveal these superficies in proliferation and with meticulous precision. But he wants also to look within the minds of his upperclass personages, in order that he may reveal the kind of suffering which must needs result from the activity of such sociological factors.

O'Hara, expressing as he does so implicitly in his work the conclusiveness of the "private hell" theory, makes of being rich a new dimension in the fiction of the past thirty years. It is the portrayal of social class distinction as the causative factor in the "private hell" to be endured by rich and poor alike.

NOTES

1. "Pottsville, Pennsylvania," *Encyclopaedia Britannica* (Chicago, London, Toronto: Encyclopaedia Britannica, Inc., 1957), XVIII, 376.
2. Lewis Nichols, "Interview with John O'Hara," in New York *Times* Book Review, November 27, 1955, p. 26.
3. Letter from John O'Hara to the writer, June 21, 1958.
4. Edmund Wilson, *The Boys in the Back Room* (San Francisco: The Colt Press, 1941), p. 18.
5. *Appointment in Samarra* (New York: Modern Library, 1934), p. 65.
6. Ibid., p. 5.
7. Robert Gorham Davis, Review of *Ten North Frederick,* New York *Times* Book Review, November 27, 1955, p. 22.
8. Arthur Mizener, "American Fiction . . . ," *Perspectives,* Spring, 1955.
9. Letter from John O'Hara, June 21, 1958.
10. *Sweet and Sour* (New York: Random House, 1956), p. 155.
11. *Ten North Frederick,* p. 105.
12. Ibid., p. 245.
13. *Appointment in Samarra,* p. 259.
14. Lewis Nichols, *loc. cit.*
15. *Ten North Frederick,* p. 148.
16. Ibid., p. 190.
17. Ibid., p. 245.
18. Ibid., p. 9.
19. Wilson, *loc. cit.*
20. *Appointment in Samarra,* p. 219.
21. Delmore Schwartz, Review of Fifty Stories from the *New Yorker* Magazine, *Partisan Review,* June, 1950, p. 294.
22. *Appointment in Samarra,* Foreword, p. xix.
23. Schwartz, *op. cit.,* June, 1950, pp. 294 ff.
24. Wilson, *op. cit.,* p. 18.
25. Ibid.
26. Harvey Breit, Review of "A Rage to Live," *Atlantic Monthly,* September, 1949, p. 84.
27. Ibid.

28. Lee Rogow, Review of "A Rage to Live," *Saturday Review* of Literature, August 20, 1949, p. 11.
29. John Woodburn, Review of "A Rage to Live," *The New Republic,* October 31, 1949, p. 18.
30. Ibid.
31. Breit, *op. cit.,* p. 84.
32. Ibid.
33. Davis, New York *Times* Book Review, p. 1.
34. St. Clair McKelway, Review in *New Yorker* Magazine, December 17, 1955, p. 162.
35. *Time* Magazine, November 28, 1955, p. 66.
36. Leslie Fiedler, Article in *The New Republic,* January 9, 1956, p. 16.
37. Davis, *loc. cit.*
38. David Boroff, *Saturday Review* of Literature, February 12, 1960, p. 27.
39. W. H. Auden, *In Memory of W. B. Yeats.*
40. Lionel Trilling, Introduction to *The Selected Short Stories of John O'Hara* (New York: Random House, 1957).
41. Ibid.
42. Ibid.
43. *Summer's Day.*
44. Wilson, *loc. cit.*
45. *The Short Stories of F. Scott Fitzgerald,* ed. Malcolm Cowley (New York: Charles Scribner's Sons, 1951).
46. Ernest Hemingway, *The Collected Short Stories* (New York: Charles Scribner's Sons, 1955).
47. Wilson, *op. cit.,* p. 22.
48. Trilling, *op. cit.*

BIBLIOGRAPHY

Auden, W. H. *In Memory of W. B. Yeats.*

Boroff, David. *Saturday Review* of Literature, February 12, 1960, p. 27.

Breit, Harvey. Review of "A Rage to Live," *Atlantic Monthly,* September, 1949, p. 84.

Davis, Robert Gorham. Review of "Ten North Frederick," New York *Times* Book Review, November 27, 1955, pp. 1, 22.

Fiedler, Leslie. Article in *The New Republic,* January 9, 1956, p. 16.

Hemingway, Ernest. *The Collected Short Stories.* New York: Charles Scribner's Sons, 1955.

Letter from John O'Hara to the writer, March 26, 1958.

Letter from John O'Hara to the writer, June 21, 1958.

McKelway, St. Clair. Review in *New Yorker* Magazine, December 17, 1955, p. 162.

Mizener, Arthur. "American Fiction . . . ," *Perspectives,* Spring, 1955.

Nichols, Lewis. "Interview with John O'Hara," New York *Times* Book Review, November 27, 1955, p. 26.

O'Hara, John. *Appointment in Samarra.* New York: Modern Library, 1934.

———. *A Rage to Live.* New York: Random House, 1949.

———. *Sweet and Sour.* New York: Random House, 1956.

———. *Ten North Frederick.* New York: Random House, 1955.

"Pottsville, Pennsylvania," *Encyclopaedia Britannica.* Chicago, London, Toronto: Encyclopaedia Britannica, Inc., 1957, XVIII, 376.

Rogow, Lee. Review of "A Rage to Live," *Saturday Review* of Literature, August 20, 1949, p. 11.

Schwartz, Delmore. Review of Fifty Stories from the *New Yorker* Magazine, *Partisan Review,* June, 1950, pp. 294 ff.

The Short Stories of F. Scott Fitzgerald, ed. Malcolm Cowley. New York: Charles Scribner's Sons, 1951.

Time Magazine, November 28, 1955, p. 66.

Wilson, Edmund. *The Boys in the Back Room.* San Francisco: The Colt Press, 1941.

Woodburn, John. Review of *A Rage to Live, The New Republic,* October 31, 1949, p. 18.

DATE DUE